30th ANNIVERSARY

Through The Years

CILLA BLACK

30th ANNIVERSARY

Through The Years

My Life In Pictures

EDITED BY TONY BARROW

HEADLINE

To Mam
Thank you for your sense of humour
Thank you for your strength
And thank you for being you

First published in 1993 by
HEADLINE BOOK PUBLISHING LTD

10 9 8 7 6 5 4 3 2 1

British Library Cataloguing in Publication Data

Black, Cilla
    Through the years
    I. Title
    791.092

        ISBN 0-7472-0918-9 (hardback)

        ISBN 0-7472-7878-4 (softback)

Book Interior by Design/Section
Illustration reproduction by Koford, Singapore
Printed and bound in Great Britain by Butler and Tanner Limited, Frome

HEADLINE BOOK PUBLISHING LTD
Headline House
79 Great Titchfield Street
London W1P 7FN

Contents

Memories are Made of Words and Music **7**

Part 1: the sixties

1963 White Becomes Black **14**

1964 Coming of Age **20**

1965 Down Under and All Over **28**

1966 Chatter on the Box........................**34**

1967 Managing Change **40**

1968 In Front of the Cameras **44**

1969 Wedding Bells **48**

Part 2: the seventies

1970 Mum's the Word **56**

1971 Two Roberts...................................**60**

1972 I Do Like to be Beside the Seaside ...**64**

1973 Party Time **66**

1974 Enter Ben **70**

1975 Casa Roll..**74**

1976 Cilla at the Palace **78**

1977 Bye Bye Beeb.................................**84**

1978 Princess Cilla **86**

1979 Roots **90**

Part 3: the eighties

1980 And Jack Makes Three......................**94**

1981 The Natural Red-Head **98**

1982 Bobby's Girl **102**

1983 Twenty Years On **104**

1984 A New Venture **110**

Surprise, Surprise..................................**114**

1985 Playing Cupid **116**

1986 A Flair for Panto..........................**120**

1987 Prize-Winning Personality **122**

1988 Silver Jubilee...............................**124**

1989 The Name of the Rose **126**

Part 4: the nineties

1990 Panda-ing to the Aussies **130**

Blind Date..**134**

1991 Buying a Hat **138**

1992 Thirty Years Younger **142**

1993 A New Look.................................**146**

UK Discography....................................**157**

Acknowledgements

Concept and Direction: Rick Blaskey/The Music & Media Partnership
Research and Picture Editor: Simon Carter/The Music & Media Partnership
Editorial Associate: Judith Simons

Creative Consultants: Bobby Willis, John Ashby
Additional Research: Sarah Evans, Nick Fiveash
Special Thanks: Jane Trafford
With Thanks To: Gary Shoefield, Shane Chapman (LWT), Bobbie Mitchell
(BBC), Dave Beecham (Rex Features), Elaine English (Hulton Deutsch),
Norman Davies (Scope Features)

Additional Acknowledgements: Jonathan Bell, Phil Chamberlain, Jan Ford,
Gary Hinchcliffe, Colin Matley, Paul Mellor, Ken Richardson, Keith Shepherd,
Helen Wild, Ray Williams

Main Cover Photograph: Photographer – John Swannell, Hair – Leslie Russell
at Smile, Make-up – Arianne Poole, Stylist - Stephen Adnitt

With regard to the BBC photographs, every effort has been made to obtain
approval from third parties.

Cilla Black's new album 'Through The Years' is released by
Sony Records

Memories are made of words and music

Whenever somebody mentions a song from the past which is a favourite of mine, or I hear it being played on the radio, precious memories come flooding back. I hope this book will have the same effect on you. Ask me what I was doing forty, twenty or even ten years ago and I'll remember absolutely nothing, or I'll have to look it up – but play me a pop record I was really fond of at the time and the tune is likely to jog my memory. Music helps us all to recall friends and relive special occasions from our past.

As I went through all the photographs, scrapbooks, concert programmes and pieces of personal memorabilia which are a part of this book, I found my favourite songs from each year going round in my head. Why is it that we can remember every line of lyrics from songs we first heard thirty or forty years ago, but not the words of records that were on Top of the Pops last month?

The songs that meant most to me when I was very young, when I was growing up in Liverpool, often conjure up the most vivid mental pictures of all, reminding me of marvellous childhood friendships and adventures, the good times, the best times – and the occasional bad times. I expect it's the same for you.

How did you listen to your earliest pop music? On a juke-box in a coffee bar or on a Dansette record-player in your big brother's bedroom while he was out on a date? On a tinny little trannie you hid in your handbag or on an old bakelite wireless your parents shoved away under the stairs when they bought the telly? Did you listen to Radio Luxemburg in the fifties, Radio Caroline in the sixties or Radio 1 in the seventies? Or are you just a babe who's growing up with Richard Branson's kind of commercial radio in the nineties?

I was born in 1943, after the Second World War blitzing of Merseyside was over, and grew up in the Liverpool of the fifties, in a two-up two-down on Scotland Road, above a barber's shop, behind a branch of Midland Bank and next door to a Chinese laundry. There was a pub on every street corner on both sides of Scottie Road and the whole area had a pretty bad reputation as the roughest residential part of town. But I felt totally safe and completely protected, even as a teenage girl walking home on my own down Scotland Road after dark.

Despite the semi-derelict state of some bomb-damaged buildings around us, we weren't actually short of space – our main living-room in Scotland Road was as large as the lounge of the house I've lived in at Denham since 1969. My brothers and I had our own bedrooms, although the loo was outside and the council didn't put in a bathroom until I was eleven. Before that we used to fill a tin bath in front of the kitchen fire from buckets of hot water heated on the stove.

Much of the earliest jazz and pop music I heard at home came out of a great big radiogram, more a centrepiece of living-room furniture than a mere record-player. It took ten records at a time, 10 or 12-inch 78s which it slapped down on to the turntable one by one. A heavy pick-up arm swung across into place and dropped like a brick on to the grooves, often missing the opening bars. My two older brothers, John and George, used to play Dean Martin and Frank Sinatra records. I was very 'hip' and knew the latest pop hits. I won threepence (in old money) by singing 'When the Moon Hits Your Eyes' ['That's Amore'] in a school contest.

When I was thirteen years old, I wrote to America for the autographs of Dean Martin and Jerry Lewis, and I was mad about Frankie Lymon who fronted The Teenagers. He was a year older than me. I liked older men. I copied him, I wanted to be him. I drove my family mad by playing his few hits every day at four o'clock as soon as I came home from school. I'd go into the bathroom where there was a good echo and I'd sing 'Why Do Fools Fall in Love?' or 'I'm Not a Juvenile Delinquent' in front of the mirror.

My father worked mostly nights as a docker and I can still hear him saying: 'Can't you keep that child quiet, I've got to be at work at ten!' My mother would be very reasonable with me: 'Can you leave off until next week, luv, when he's on days again?' To this day I could still do you a fair impression of Frankie Lymon.

My friend Chris borrowed her mother's mail-order catalogue and we bought blue jeans which cost us 1s 3d a week. The blue jeans were our uniform, just like Frankie Lymon's group. Imagine how excited we were when he and his Teenagers came to Liverpool *in person* for concerts at the Empire Theatre in Lime Street and stayed at the Lord Nelson Hotel. For a dare, I actually got the maid who was cleaning Frankie Lymon's bedroom to give me the contents of his wastepaper basket. It contained the US equivalent of an Equity card which had belonged to Frankie, and I kept and treasured it for many years.

Even when we were a bit older, as a rule we couldn't afford tickets for the Empire unless we saved up for ages, but we managed the occasional night out at a dance hall on Sundays, the Locarno or Grafton Ballroom, or maybe Orrell Park. The big romantic record of the day was

'My Prayer' by The Platters. I can picture the scene now in any of Liverpool's dance halls or coffee clubs at the end of a typical mid-fifties evening. If a fella asked you up for 'My Prayer', you were on to a good thing. Halfway through the record, invariably the last one of the evening, if he got around to asking where you lived and it wasn't somewhere daft on the other side of the Mersey like Birkenhead, that clinched it – he was planning to see you home.

I used to like all the American rhythm and blues groups but not British rock 'n' roll, because I thought it was too sanitised, even Cliff Richard. In those days you liked Elvis or Cliff, not both. The difference was that I fancied Cliff, basically he was my teenage dream and he was more accessible than Elvis, who never came over here. Again the older man, you see, because I was fifteen and Cliff was something like seventeen and a half and that's a big age gap when you're a teenager. So when I waited outside stage doors for Cliff, it wasn't because of his singing – it was raw sexuality that drew me to him. After one of his shows at the Philharmonic Hall, Liverpool, I chased a taxi I thought Cliff was in, but it turned out to be two of his Shadows and Jimmy Tarbuck, on their way to Jim's for a party.

It's no wonder that I knew I wanted to be a professional singer from a very early age, because I was surrounded by music in our house. My father played the mouth organ, my mother and my aunts used to sing, and it wasn't unusual for families to get together and make their own music in the fifties. Our John, my middle brother, played the clarinet and saxophone and could read music. We had a piano which my dad had bought from the Epstein family's local furniture stores. That's why he was quite willing to sign my management contract with Brian Epstein when I turned professional in 1963 (I was twenty and still under-age). My dad thought: 'That man's OK as Cilla's manager, he sells great pianos.' But I shouldn't leap ahead to 1963 just yet – I'm missing out some formative years.

If I'm remembering songs that were significant to me I mustn't leave out Peggy Lee's 'Fever'. At Anfield Commercial College, where they taught me to type after I left school, one of my friends was Pauline Behan, a girl who was dating George Harrison at the time but later married Gerry Marsden. Pauline took me to a club called the Iron Door in the centre of Liverpool to see one of Merseyside's most popular groups, Rory Storm and the Hurricanes, the very first group I ever sang with, but not for money. Perhaps what Pauline said carried a bit of weight among the local bands because people knew that George of The Beatles had been buying her coffee. Anyway, she asked Rory's group to give me a go at singing 'Fever' – and they did! Wally, the bass player (who looked like Buddy Holly), shoved a microphone in front of my face as if to say: 'Show us what you're made of.' Pauline got all our mates to cheer like mad. I must have done OK because not long afterwards The Big Three actually *paid* me to sing with them at a coffee place called The Zodiac, where I was billed as Swinging Cilla. (Incidentally, I met Bobby at The Zodiac when I was eighteen and he was nineteen, although he claimed he was older because he'd heard I liked older men.)

The gig with The Big Three was a try-out more than anything else. I couldn't have taken a singing job with the group on a regular basis because I was working as a typist at a cable

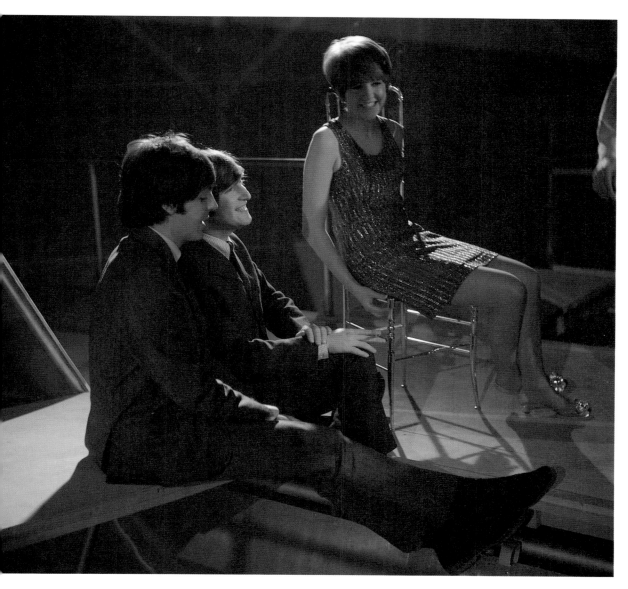

On the set of The Beatles: The Music of Lennon and McCartney on 1 November 1965: Cilla with John and Paul. 'When I recorded 'It's For You' in 1964, John and Paul came along to the recording session the same day they arrived back from Australia. George Martin told them they'd better wait outside because I was nervous and he was right. I was always nervous when I was recording!

'But with John and Paul I didn't mind. They often dropped in when I was in the studios, and anyway I was glad to see them back safely from Australia. Paul had introduced me to 'It's For You' with a demo disc which he made himself and sent round to the Palladium for me. George Martin took a big hand in the recording of it, writing the arrangement and directing the orchestra as well as supervising the session. Although Paul sang it as a waltz on the demo disc, George put in the jazzy bits for the session arrangement. It was different from what I'd done before.' *(Scope Features)*

**Opening night party of *Sugar Babies*, September
1988, with husband Bobby Willis.**

(Syndication International)

company by then. But I did appear with
Kingsize Taylor and the Dominoes because
they had day jobs like me, and only took dates
they could get to and from in their spare time.
Kingsize never told me what to sing, it was more
a question of picking stuff we all knew,
throwing song titles at each other until
something matched. But we all liked the same
type of material, basically rock 'n' roll, so we
got on well.

Now we're up to 1963 and this, as they say,
is where the story *really* begins. If you read
between the lines as we go *through the years*,
you'll realise that I'm as big a fan of
showbusiness today as I was when I hung
around the stage door of the Liverpool Empire
hoping for a glimpse of Frankie Lymon and the
Teenagers in the fifties. That's why I got such a
kick out of having my own favourite stars like
Jerry Lewis and Bob Hope on my early BBC
television shows, and why I'm over the moon
now about having such smashing guests as
Dusty Springfield, Barry Manilow and ever-so-

sexy Cliff Richard to sing with me on my new thirtieth anniversary album. The words and the
pictures we've put together on the pages which follow are not intended to be a full-scale
autobiography. I don't want to think about writing that until I retire. Instead, here is a
collection of memories, laced with a lorra songs, which together tell the story of my first thirty
years in showbusiness, 1963 to 1993.

PART 1

the sixties

1963

WHITE BECOMES BLACK

HIGHLIGHTS

30 AUGUST	**Concert debut, Odeon, Southport, with The Beatles**
6 SEPTEMBER	**Signs with Brian Epstein**
25 SEPTEMBER	**TV debut on Discs A Go Go**
27 SEPTEMBER	**'Love of the Loved' released**
28 SEPTEMBER	**Appears in the 'hot seat' on Juke Box Jury**
4 OCTOBER	**1st UK concert tour with Gerry and the Pacemakers, 32 dates**
5 OCTOBER	**Appears on Thank Your Lucky Stars**
23 NOVEMBER	**5 concert tour with Billy J. Kramer and the Dakotas**
24 DECEMBER	**Appears in The Beatles Christmas Show, Astoria, Finsbury Park, London**

Cilla's earliest publicity centred on a simple slogan: The Black bird is coming. Follow-up press releases described her as The Gal with the Bright Red Hair and the Jet Black Voice and dubbed her The Only Bird in a Beat Boys' World.

This was September 1963, and a twenty-year-old Liverpudlian typist named Priscilla Maria Veronica White had waved 'tarrah' to office workmates at an insulated cable manufacturing company and told them that she was off to London for a holiday. In fact she had signed a management contract with The Beatles' mentor, local record retailer Brian Epstein, and turned into a professional singer called Cilla Black. Various versions of the name-change story have appeared over the years. The truth is that Epstein believed white was a weak-sounding word while black suited the girl's vocal image: rhythmic, bluesy and leathery-black. Cilla went along with that.

'Love of the Loved' –

the first single. *(EMI Records)*

On the scene at The Cavern: Cilla and Gerry twistin' the night away.

(Tony Barrow)

Hearing Cilla had left a typing job in Liverpool to become a full-time professional singer, press photographers couldn't wait to get her behind a typewriter again. She posed helpfully at a desk in her publicist's London office. *(Rex Features)*

NEMS ENTERPRISES LTD

PRESS OFFICE: 13, MONMOUTH STREET, LONDON W.C.2.   TELEPHONE COVent Gds 2332

"The *Black bird* is *coming!*"

'The Black bird is coming' – NEMS press release, September.

(Tony Barrow)

Cilla

My full name was Priscilla Maria Veronica White and because my mum's name was Priscilla too, she was known as Big Priscilla and I was Little Priscilla. In the area I came from having a posh name like that was very embarrassing.

Brian Epstein was exceedingly proud of his latest discovery, the first female artiste to join the roster of all-male Merseybeat groups represented by his recently launched management firm, NEMS (North End Music Stores) Enterprises. But 'Eppy' was slow to share credit for his discovery with John Lennon, although it was The Beatles' unofficial leader who had brought the promising young singing talent of Swinging Cilla to his notice in the first place.

Cilla swung into London clutching a well-worn vanity case which rattled with bottles of cosmetics and declared that she kept her face in there and wouldn't go anywhere without it ('I look quite ill without my blusher'). She made no attempt to hide the fact that one of the bottles held the secret to her bright red hair: 'I've dyed it ever since I was fourteen when I bought my first hair colouring from Woolies.'

Cilla

As a teenager in Liverpool I wanted to be smart, and as I couldn't get the clothes I wanted off the peg I learned to make my own things. They didn't last very long!

Naturally enough, Cilla's manager took her to EMI record producer George Martin, the man who had made The Beatles' first hits and helped Gerry and the Pacemakers to have three Number 1 singles in a row. Cilla was impressed with her first sessions at Abbey Road. 'George has got a really deep feeling for Liverpool music and he's wonderful in the studio,' she said.

At the time, the NEMS publicity machinery let it appear that Lennon and McCartney had custom-tailored the song 'Love of the Loved' for Cilla's first record. She told the press: 'I've

Cilla sitting on the bandstand at The Cavern with her best Liverpudlian buddy, pal and mate, Pat Davies: the two girls were close from childhood days when they shared an ambition to become hairdressers because it sounded glamorous and they'd get their own styling done free. Later in London Pat worked in the music business while Cilla established herself as an entertainer and they lunched and went shopping together. After Cilla and Bobby married, Pat was such a frequent and welcome visitor to their Denham home that she held her own set of house keys, unofficially filling in for the family's nanny whenever necessary and 'house-sitting' while they were away. Ten years ago Pat married an American television executive and went to live in New York but she and Cilla have stayed in touch: 'Pat has been a wonderful friend to us all, and she has a heart of gold.' *(Hulton Deutsch)*

(Left) Strangers in town: Cilla and Bobby in Regent's Park on their first visit to London in 1963. 'If Bobby hadn't been willing to give up his bakery job in Liverpool to travel with me and look after me my parents would never have let me leave home and try my luck in showbusiness.' *(Rex Features/David Magnus)*

(Right) Cilla on tour: backstage with Billy J. Kramer towards the end of 1963. *(Rex Features/Dezo Hoffmann)*

(Left) 'Who's Who in Show Biz' Annual, late 1963/early 1964.

NEW MUSICAL EXPRESS

Friday, October 18, 1963

New to the Charts **Cilla Black**

RED-HEADED Cilla Black becomes the first Merseypop girl singer to hit the charts with her debut disc, "Love Of The Loved." It is an up-tempo number specially written for her by Beatles John Lennon and Paul McCartney.

Born on May 27, 1943, Cilla's real name is Priscilla Maria Veronica White. She's an attractive 5 ft. 5 in. tall, with dark blue eyes that she says "go black at night!"

NME 'New to the Charts' profile, 18 October.(*NME*)

Cilla left St. Anthony's Secondary Modern School, Liverpool, in July, 1958, and began a course at a secretarial college. At the end of 1959 she joined the staff of a Liverpool firm as a typist.

In the evenings she became a "regular" at Liverpool's famed Cavern Club. "I used to spend four evenings a week there," she says.

"One night, some friends arranged for one of the vocalists to pass down the mike just for a joke. I had to take up the lyrics of 'Fever' where he left off. Then they made me go up on the stage and sing 'Always,' and some r-and-b things. That was three years ago.

"Afterwards, I got to know all the big groups like the Beatles and Gerry and the Pacemakers, and we used to have these marvellous jam sessions together."

Cilla's likes include swimming, curries, Paul Newman, dancing the Cavern Stomp, tall boys who are "as mad as I am," and sunbathing in her bikini.

She says she doesn't like people who slurp their tea, slingback shoes which slip, and waiting in queues ! ALAN SMITH.

realised one of my biggest ambitions already – it was to have a song written for me by John and Paul of The Beatles.'

In fact Cilla had heard them doing the number as part of their stage act at The Cavern and knew it wasn't brand new. The main point was that it suited her, even if it was off the peg. The pop music world of the early sixties was full of such little white lies. Epstein was, for example, obsessively particular about the private lives of his stars and hated to let their personal affairs become public knowledge. They had to hide their loves away, keep their partners out of the limelight. Since Cilla was the only female on his books, 'Eppy' had no experience of keeping boyfriends in the background (except his own).

In Cilla's case, a young Liverpool baker, Bobby Willis, was absolutely the only man in her uncomplicated love-life. He was one year older than her ('I liked older men'). To account for his constant presence at her side and simply to avoid any awkward questions, Cilla agreed that Bobby should be her road manager. He took the job very seriously, lost little time teaching himself the ropes of the music business and became a first-class roadie.

On the B-side of Cilla's debut single she sang 'Shy of Love'.

Cilla

Until the day before my first recording session I never realised I had such a talented road manager. That was when Bobby Willis showed me a song he'd written called 'Shy of Love'. Everyone at the session thought it was good enough to go on the second side of the single although it was Bobby's first attempt.

Cilla's earliest UK concert tour was a month-long series of one-nighters in cinemas and theatres around the country with Gerry and the Pacemakers, culminating at the Liverpool Empire. Before she went out on the road with Gerry, a week before her formal signature with 'Eppy', Cilla had done an unpublicised 'sneak preview' performance in Southport with The Beatles. The date came about by accident rather than design: she was filling in for another

NEMS act, The Fourmost, who were pulled out of the date at the eleventh hour to do a valuable national television 'plug', a spot on ITV's Ready Steady Go in London.

After 1963, it's fair to say that Cilla's career shot forward and upwards at high speed under its own impetus, but she is the first to admit that many of her most important bookings in the immediate wake of her recording debut came as a direct result of her association with The Beatles, Brian Epstein and the powerful new NEMS Enterprises.

After less than four months as a full-time professional, Cilla rounded off the year with a three-week London season in The Beatles Christmas Show at the Astoria Theatre, Finsbury Park (later renamed The Rainbow).

Cilla

At the opening of The Beatles Christmas Show at Finsbury Park Astoria, London, in December 1963 everybody else seemed dead nervous and they all wondered why I seemed so confident. I'll tell you what it was – a glass of champagne for courage. And it's worked for me ever since!

'When I saw myself on the big screen for the first time doing a guest appearance in Gerry Marsden's film *Ferry Cross the Mersey*, I just stood up and screamed. The song I performed in that movie, 'Is It Love?' was written by Bobby. He also wrote the B-sides of my first two records. He should have stuck with his composing.' *(Hulton Deutsch)*

(Right) Typical NEMS 'handout' shot for the press linked two Epstein acts in one picture: Santa Cilla gives Christmas presents to Gerry and the Pacemakers. *(Tony Barrow)*

1964

COMING OF AGE

HIGHLIGHTS

31 JANUARY	**'Anyone Who Had a Heart' released**
21 FEBRUARY	**'Anyone Who Had a Heart' No. 1 in *NME* chart**
29 FEBRUARY	**Concert tour of England, 36 dates**
23 MARCH	**1st Silver Disc, for 'Anyone Who Had a Heart'**
APRIL	**EP 'Anyone Who Had a Heart' released**
20 APRIL	**1 week residency, Palace Theatre, Manchester**
26 APRIL	***NME* poll-winners' show, Empire Pool, Wembley**
1 MAY	**'You're My World' released**
6 MAY	**Appears on Around The Beatles TV special**
13 MAY	**Startime season, London Palladium**
27 MAY	**21st birthday**
23 JULY	**Appears in Night of 100 Stars charity show, London Palladium**
31 JULY	**'It's for You' released**
OCTOBER	**EP 'It's For You' released**
2 NOVEMBER	**Appears on Royal Variety Show**
6 DECEMBER	**Film *Ferry Cross the Mersey* opens**

In the fifties and sixties, the London Palladium was considered the world's top variety theatre. It was the ultimate aim of every performer to get a booking there. Most singers, comics, jugglers and magicians spent half their careers waiting and hoping for such a break. Dancers auditioned in their hundreds for each new Palladium show. The biggest American names in the business queued up to top the bill there and ITV produced a star-studded hour-long spectacular, Sunday Night at the London Palladium, televised live from the famous West End venue each weekend.

On 13 May 1964, less than eight months after her launch, Cilla opened at the Palladium in Startime on a bill headed by Frankie Vaughan and Tommy Cooper,

with The Fourmost among the supporting acts. The show was planned as a short season but its run was extended because of unexpectedly heavy business at the box office. Between May and December Cilla did thirteen shows a week at the Palladium, a total of over 400 performances.

Cilla

In May 1964 our families took the train south to see me at the Palladium. There was a gang of Whites, my relatives, and a handful of Bobby's folks all sitting in the dining car together. When the waiter came round with the coffee he asked, 'Are you all whites?' Bobby's brother replied, 'No, three of us are Willises'. When I went on tour with the groups in the sixties I'd come back to the hotel after a show to find the boys had filled the lift with flowers for me. It was marvellous – except that I was worried stiff because I

(Above) Startime at the London Palladium, May/December – poster. 'My first London Palladium season started in May 1964 and I was on a bill with Tommy Cooper and Frankie Vaughan. Down in London the Palladium was regarded with a sort of awe and reverence, but back home in the North it's just another theatre. I realised later that it was a landmark in my career but I didn't look on it as the ultimate at the time.'

(Right) 'Because I understand fans, I don't sneak out of side entrances or use getaway cars, I think that would be cheating.' (Rex Features)

(Left) Melody Maker chart, 29 February, 'Anyone Who Had a Heart' at Number 1. 'Bacharach wasn't the be-all and end-all of everything. I just felt there was a little bit of magic on our record and that was proved when it came out. Dionne Warwick's record was released and it got nowhere. Three weeks later mine went to Number 1 and was selling nearly 100,000 a day, so it had a touch of magic.' (Melody Maker)

(Top) 'Anyone Who Had a Heart' – sheet music. *(Carlin Music)* (Centre) 'It's For You' – EP cover. (Bottom) *Photoplay* cover, September.

knew they hadn't bought them. They'd pinched them from all round the hotel. When I signed with Brian I did 400 live performances in eight months. I couldn't do that now. I'd have to train for it. I didn't appreciate how lucky I was to be young and have stamina and good health. I used to live on chip butties, frozen hamburgers and fish fingers and never put on weight.

Later on I tried to eat the proper foods, but it just wasn't possible when I was working in a show or rehearsing. Inevitably, we ended up eating snacks, or even nothing at all. So I would take a soluble vitamin supplement every day.

The way had been paved for Cilla's Palladium booking by the success of her second single, 'Anyone Who Had a Heart', which took her to the top of the charts in February, making her the first female to hit the Number 1 spot since Helen Shapiro and 'Walking Back to Happiness' in October 1961. The achievement was all the more special because so-called Beatlemania had broken out in Britain since the release of 'Love of the Loved' and the pop scene had become dominated by groups to the almost total exclusion of solo singers. Nor was Cilla the only person to release a recording of the Burt Bacharach-Hal David ballad.

During a trip to New York, Brian Epstein heard the original version of 'Anyone Who Had a Heart' sung by Dionne Warwick. On his return to London, he gave a

'You're My World' – sheet music. **'When I reached Number 1 in the charts with 'You're My World', it made me the first British girl to have two successive Number 1 hits. I heard the good news just days before my twenty-first birthday. Two Number 1 hits in a row ... absurd! I'd been wondering if it would happen all through the previous week, but having reached Number 2, I thought I might stick there.** **'We had a little "do" at home to celebrate. We opened a bottle of champagne The Beatles gave me at Christmas. Brian Epstein, who gave me a gold watch for my first Number 1 hit, asked me if I liked mink, but I said "No, I hate it'."** *(Carlin Music)*

copy to George Martin. At the time George was reported to have agreed at once that the song would be perfect for Cilla. In fact he said: 'Brian, it's a lovely song. It's absolutely ideal for Shirley.' 'Eppy' kept his cool and replied flatly, 'I wasn't thinking of Shirley Bassey.'

The EMI recording manager doubted that Cilla could cope with such an emotional piece and Cilla herself said, 'I didn't think it would stand a chance, but it was such a gorgeous record that I couldn't let the chance go by.' Johnny Pearson scored the Bacharach song, using a lush string section and powerful rhythm, exchanging the piano on the Warwick original for an organ and putting in a distinctive French horn sound. George Martin was convinced that from the

orchestral point of view he had a much better sound, but it was Cilla's vocal treatment that turned the finished product into a Number 1 hit. Johnny Pearson, who directed the orchestra for 'Anyone Who Had a Heart' and 'You're My World', said this of Cilla in *Disc* magazine in 1964: 'She's a perfectionist and the biggest critic of herself. I've a tremendous admiration for Cilla as a singer and as a person. I think she's nervous on sessions, but she never conveys it to other people working with her.

'She knows exactly what she wants, and is very quick to tell you about it. Quite often she comes up with a suggestion which improves and puts the finishing touch on the song we're cutting. She's got a very swift brain and she's perceptive and constructive without a trace of temperament.

'She walks through difficult passages without any apparent trouble. Yet sometimes she gets mad with herself over a minor point which she thinks she can do better. And she's always smart – no matter what time the session or how long it lasts.'

When Cilla heard she was top of the pops she couldn't contain her delight.

Cilla

I said, 'You know what? This afternoon I'm going to have a posh hair-do, then I'm going round to BICC' – the cable firm where I used to work in Liverpool – 'I'll see all my mates and tell my old boss I'm a star!'

Around The Beatles: on the set of Jack Good's television special. 'One of my earliest memories of doing television dates back to 1963 in Southampton. It was only my second time on TV and they told me to dance. I danced right past the camera and there was a blank screen for about ten seconds.'
(Scope Features)

(Above) Cilla with The Beatles, Billy J. Kramer and the Dakotas and The Searchers on Thank Your Lucky Stars. *(Redferns)*

(Above right) Ready, steady, break! – Cilla and George Martin chat between Ready, Steady, Go rehearsals. *(Rex Features)*

(Right) July 1964: record producer George Martin explains a point to Cilla as Bobby Willis (left) looks on. 'When I first did an audition at EMI, we were in the big studio; it was the one in which you had to climb up a lot of stairs into the producer's control box. I recorded 'Love of the Loved' which Paul McCartney had written, I'd often heard him doing it at the lunchtime sessions in The Cavern and I thought this is smashing, this is lovely. In the studio I was confronted for the first time with real musicians, you know, with music, which I wasn't used to at all. I wanted a really good club band sound, a real group sound, a Cavern sound. EMI's Abbey Road studios had a very clinical atmosphere; it wasn't very enjoyable at all. But when I hear it today, I think it's really smashing.' *(EMI Records)*

(Left) 'Cilla Swings in with a Second Smash Single!' – NEMS press release.

(Right) Cilla posed for pictures on a winter's day in Shaftesbury Avenue: The Fab Four were bosom friends and held close to Cilla's heart. *(Rex Features)*

(Left) Cilla, Brian Epstein and her Silver Disc, awarded for sales of 'Anyone Who Had a Heart' in excess of 250,000 copies. Brian Epstein on Cilla Black in his book *A Cellarful of Noise*, referring to signing her in September 1963: 'I first heard her sing with The Beatles in Birkenhead but had not been greatly impressed because the acoustics had been wrong for her voice, but the next occasion was early one morning in The Blue Angel Club in Liverpool. She looked, as always, magnificent – a slender, graceful creature with the ability to shed her mood of dignified repose if she were singing a fast number. I watched her move and I watched her stand and I half-closed my eyes and imagined her on a vast stage with the right lighting. I was convinced she could become a wonderful artiste.'
(Hulton Deutsch)

(Below) They met backstage at the London Palladium on 20 May 1964 and Dionne Warwick said to Cilla: 'I think your version of 'Anyone Who Had a Heart' was simply great.' This disappointed the press who had hoped the ladies would have a verbal punch-up over rival recordings of the same hit.

'When I was just Priscilla White, typist, singing at The Cavern for a giggle, that loud raucous voice was the only way I could sing. The first record I ever made, 'Love of the Loved' used that voice entirely and I still think it was a good record. It was after that, when I'd been out on a few tours and George Martin asked me to record Dionne Warwick's 'Anyone Who Had a Heart', that the softer voice developed.'
(Syndication International)

Cilla's success was at the expense of Dionne Warwick, whose original version of 'Anyone Who Had a Heart' whipped in and out of the UK best-sellers. The Crystals, in London for a tour, condemned Cilla's 'cover' in no uncertain terms. 'It would be different if she had done the song her way, but to take it from somebody else and do their every move is not right,' said Crystal Dee Dee Kenniebrew. 'It seems a strain for her to reach the high notes, whereas Dionne does it with ease.' Cilla refused to get too involved in the controversy, replying simply: 'I'd probably say the same.'

Some of the mud slung by Dionne Warwick's fans might have stuck if Cilla had not consolidated her position as the leading new recording star of the year with a swift return to the top of the charts. Her third single, 'You're My World', reached Number 1 in May, coinciding with her birthday. Cilla celebrated her twenty-first birthday on the stage of the London Palladium amid a barrage of press publicity: 'I'll never be able to lie about my age now!' she joked.

Backstage at the London Palladium for Night of 100 Stars, 23 July. 'I love going on stage and I'm never nervous. I'm like a racehorse waiting to go into the Grand National, pawing the ground, waiting to get at it!'

(Syndication International)

Her next single, Lennon and McCartney's 'It's For You', notched up an exceedingly healthy advance order of 200,000 copies and climbed into the Top Ten, but it failed to give her a third consecutive chart-topper. 'I couldn't keep getting a Number 1 every time, people'd think I was a freak,' said Cilla. In *New Musical Express* record reviewer Derek Johnson wrote: 'She has lost much of the harshness which characterised her previous releases.'

Apart from appearing at the Palladium six nights a week, Cilla packed half a dozen Sunday concerts into her hectic schedule and sang 'You're My World' in the 1964 Royal Variety Performance, staged at the Palladium in the presence of the Queen.

In December, Cilla made her cinema debut when *Ferry Cross the Mersey*, starring Gerry and the Pacemakers, had its premiere at London's New Victoria (now the Apollo Victoria). To shoot her brief guest appearance in Gerry's musical film Cilla had made a nostalgic day-return journey to one of her teenage home-town haunts, Liverpool's Locarno Ballroom, where she sang a romantic ballad, 'Is It Love?', written for the occasion by Bobby Willis.

(Left) Cilla's happy twenty-first birthday party at the Palladium. 'In May 1964 I told people I didn't want to be twenty-one really. It'd been so fantastic being twenty. Voting was something I was looking forward to. I said I thought the voting age should be put forward to eighteen, because that's the age young people became really interested in politics. Myself, I was a Socialist at heart, but where my taxes are concerned I'm a Tory.' (Syndication International)

(Below centre) Brian Epstein helps Cilla celebrate her twenty-first birthday at the London Palladium on 27 May 1964. (Syndication International)

(Below left) 'I couldn't keep getting a Number 1 every time.'
(Rex Features/Dezo Hoffmann)

(Above) Cilla with Jimmy Savile at a Variety Club luncheon in London on 16 September 1964.
(Rex Features)

(Left) Chatting in the stalls between rehearsals for the 1964 Royal Variety Show at the London Palladium: Cilla with Millicent Martin (centre) and Kathy Kirby.
(Syndication International)

1965

DOWN UNDER AND ALL OVER

HIGHLIGHTS

8 JANUARY	**'You've Lost That Lovin' Feelin' released**
25 JANUARY	**1st album, 'Cilla', released**
29 JANUARY	**1st headline tour of UK, 22 dates**
8 MARCH	**Receives Mecca Carl-Alan award**
8 MARCH	**Concert tour of New Zealand, 7 dates, and Australia, 5 dates**
4 APRIL	**American TV debut on The Ed Sullivan Show**
11 APRIL	***New Musical Express* poll-winners' show, Empire Pool, Wembley**
15 APRIL	**'I've Been Wrong Before' released**
25 MAY	**Concert debut in France, Paris Olympia Theatre**
31 MAY	**Cabaret debut, La Dolce Vita, Newcastle**
26 JULY	**US cabaret debut, Plaza Hotel, New York**
8 OCTOBER	**Star Scene '65 UK concert tour, 18 dates**
17 DECEMBER	**Appears on The Beatles, The Music of Lennon and McCartney special**
27 DECEMBER	**Pantomime debut in *Little Red Riding Hood*, Wimbledon Theatre**

After her long season at the London Palladium was over, Cilla and Bobby flew off for a fortnight's relaxation on the sun-soaked beaches of Las Palmas in the Canary Isles, their first real getaway break since Cilla quit her job as a Liverpool typist sixteen months earlier. At the last moment the trip was delayed by several days so that Cilla could put the finishing touches to her first album and record her next single. By the end of the two-week holiday Cilla had mixed feelings.

Sleeve of 'Cilla' album. *(EMI Records)*

Cilla

Gregory Peck was arriving at our hotel as we were leaving, so I was disappointed about missing him, but I was also homesick and couldn't wait to get back to plug my new record.

Cilla in Central Park: making her debut in New York. 'I played the Persian Room in New York, which was a very posh cabaret room in the Plaza Hotel opposite Central Park. I also did the Ed Sullivan Show and the Johnny Carson Show on television. It was great walking down Fifth Avenue the next day and hearing people say "Hi Cilla, that was really great". But I was 22 and a bit too young and homesick. To crack America you really have to spend at least six months there.' *(Rex Features)*

The pressures of such speedy showbiz success, the endless round of telly spots, one-night stands and publicity sessions should have been taking their toll but Cilla was sufficiently young, fit and enthusiastic to take stardom in her stride. Indeed, 1965 proved to be her busiest year yet, beginning with a strenuous three-week UK concert tour with Sounds Incorporated, her Epstein-managed backing band.

By the beginning of 1965, with three major hits and a long string of television appearances to her credit, Cilla was a strong box-office draw at provincial concert venues, quite capable of putting plenty of bums on seats. But to give her first nationwide outing of that year extra impetus, she was co-starred with controversial American singer P. J. Proby, notorious for wearing trousers so tight (and so weakly sewn at the seams) that they tended to split around the thighs and above during his stage act. This brought him numerous newspaper headlines along with complaints from serious-minded civic authorities. Cilla said at the time: 'I was one of the first people to meet Jim when he came over from America with Jack Good to make the TV spectacular Around The Beatles, and we got on fine together.'

Days later, when theatre managements implemented an instant overnight ban on Proby because his act was considered offensive, a young Welsh singer named Tom Jones stepped in at the eleventh hour as his temporary replacement. Cilla's comment: 'In my opinion, P. J. Proby has let thousands of his fans down. He's a nice boy, why should he act like that?' But Proby's disgrace was a positive challenge for Cilla. With or without Proby, fans continued to pack houses to capacity and Cilla's latest single, 'You've Lost That Lovin' Feelin', soared in the charts (reaching Number 2 or Number 5 according to which chart you choose to follow) while her album, 'Cilla', turned into a long-term best-seller.

(Left) Cilla on stage with Sounds Incorporated. 'I didn't think 'I've Been Wrong Before' had got particular commercial appeal. I was with a gang of musicians, Sounds Incorporated actually, when I first heard it in 1965. They listened to the backing and thought it marvellous. But I listened to the voice and I thought it was hilarious. It was Randy Newman, the composer. But he also had a lot of soul. Anyway, I found I couldn't stop singing it afterwards. Randy Newman was sort of classical so far as I was concerned. He wrote things like movie themes and came from a long line of that sort of music.

'I used to go a lot on what my family said. My mother didn't like it. She wanted to know what made me record a silly thing like that. But my eighteen-year-old brother thought it was marvellous. So I told mum I was sorry – I couldn't accept her opinion.' *(Tony Barrow)*

(Right) Cilla/P.J. Proby Tour – programme cover.

(Below) Sheet music for 'You've Lost That Lovin' Feelin'. 'The version of 'You've Lost That Lovin' Feelin'' by The Righteous Brothers was 100 per cent better than mine, if only for the reason that it is not a solo record. It's a song for two people as you need two voices for that great answering thing

with the very deep voice and the very high voice. I had to do both myself and, although I have a very big range, it wasn't quite right.' *(Screen Gems/EMI Music)*

(Right) Sitting this one out? Cilla with Petula Clark (centre) and Sandie Shaw at a Variety Club luncheon for recording stars in May 1965 at London's Dorchester Hotel. *(Hulton Deutsch)*

In March 1965, Cilla undertook tours of Australia and New Zealand, where autograph-seeking fans mobbed her. 'At times like this I'm always more worried about my hat than myself,' she said. Prior to a pair of shows at Sydney Stadium, one of Cilla's supporting acts, singer Mark Wynter, unwittingly let the cat out of the bag by revealing to reporters that Cilla was 'going steady' with Bobby Willis. She indignantly denied this, insisting that Bobby's role was that of road manager, a case of telling part of the truth but not the whole of it.

In New Zealand six Maori dancers gave her a traditional welcome at the airport. When the chief went down on the ground and pulled faces at her, Cilla didn't know whether to be terrified or flattered.

Cilla

He was holding this dirty big spear and waving a fir like a Christmas tree. I had to pick it up when the dance finished and we rubbed noses together for the television cameras. They asked us to sing so we gave them 'Knees Up Mother Brown'.

With the benefit of hindsight it is clear that Cilla's launch in America was mismanaged. In April 1965 she made her debut on CBS Television's Ed Sullivan Show, America's closest equivalent to Sunday Night at the London Palladium, singing 'Dancing in the Street' and 'You're My World', and then went on Hollywood's Shindig show to sing 'I've Been Wrong Before'. To give herself half a chance of conquering such a vast territory as the USA, Cilla should have stayed over there for months. As it was, Brian Epstein had booked her for April and May television 'plugs' back in Britain, and whatever impact she might have made on the Ed Sullivan Show lacked the necessary in-person follow-up.

Brian Epstein, usually reluctant to use the bargaining power of his Beatles as a tool in his dealings on behalf of other NEMS artists, bent his own rules that summer in his passion to see Cilla crack the American market. He insisted that The Beatles' New York agents should negotiate a cabaret season for Cilla in a top Manhattan showroom. They did as they were told, but putting her into the Persian Room of the five-star Plaza Hotel in a midsummer heatwave when New York City was almost empty did little or nothing for her career. What little publicity the Americans did receive on Cilla cast her as an offshoot of The Beatles; essentially a teenage phenomenon rather than a sophisticated cabaret performer. Only those who had caught her appearance on The Johnny Carson Show had a clue about Cilla's developing abilities as an all-rounder.

Cilla

Johnny Carson said: 'Don't think I'm being rude, but I've never heard of you.' I replied: 'Don't worry, chuck, because I've never heard of you either.'

Without the right reputation and with no other suitable credentials, Cilla faced a first-night audience made up of stern media critics and indifferent diners. 'The room was full of millionaires, it scared me just to think how much it cost to eat there,' she said.

Reviews were mixed. The *Journal American* said: 'So infectious is her personality, and so loud and clear her voice, she could easily become another Gracie Fields given the proper handling.' The *World Telegram* praised her mellow and pleasing voice, drew attention to 'a charming set of slightly buck teeth that glow in the dark', and called her repertoire 'weighted with banalities'. Reports came back to Britain that 'there were almost as many waiters as there were customers' and that 'instead of 'You're My World', she sings numbers like 'Summertime', 'Bye Bye Blackbird' and, believe it or not, a medley from *My Fair Lady*'.

Cilla took what steps she could to make the best of an unenviable situation but she faced her most dangerous professional challenge to date. By her side at the Plaza were her London producer and musical director, John Lyndon, and Johnny Pearson. With their help, Cilla's act was revamped and by the end of the first week she was holding the attention of the million-dollar Persian Room clientele. At each opening she was given polite applause, but three songs later she would have most of the audience in the

(Left) Time for reflection: Cilla sitting pretty. *(London Features International)*

(Below) *NME* poll winners' concert, 11 April – programme inside bill. 'In December 1964 I was voted Britain's second most popular female singer in the *NME* poll and Dusty Springfield came top. Dusty's a marvellous singer. My father thought she was the end. Whenever I went home he always talked about Dusty. "That's what I call singing," he used to say.'(*NME*)

palm of her hand. By the final week she was giving unscheduled encores and winning over new admirers each night but she confessed in her dressing-room: 'These have been the toughest and most terrifying weeks of my life. I never thought American audiences could be so hard to please.'

The truth was that a midsummer season at the Plaza had given Cilla a very distorted and untypical view of US audiences. Unfortunately, her full diary of engagements back home prevented her from finding out more. She had impressed the producers of The Johnny Carson Show enough to earn an immediate invitation to return and do another spot, but she was unable to take up the offer until the spring of 1966. In a nutshell, Cilla's career in America began and ended with spasmodic television appearances, record releases which were not promoted in the best way and a New York cabaret stint which turned into a personal triumph but did not make her a household name. To this day Cilla regrets that her launch in America in the mid-sixties did not have more positive results, although there is every possibility that her latest project, the animation series she is creating with an impish cartoon character called Little Cilla, could hit the jackpot with the US television audiences of the mid-nineties.

Cilla at a *Melody Maker* midnight party with Ringo in January 1965. 'I'd known Ringo (Starr) since I was a kid, before I knew Bobby. And then I'd become friends with George (Harrison). But funnily it was John (Lennon) who used to push me and praise me on chat shows and things, funny because he and I were never that close. John adored women but he was never completely at home in their company, he was a man's man. Paul was the idol whom all the girls worshipped and I think John felt he was in his shadow. In order of popularity with the girls, it was Paul, John, George – and Ringo was your last resort!' *(Syndication International)*

Cilla's 1965 closed with another successful UK tour – Star Scene '65, with The Everly Brothers, Billy J. Kramer and Lionel Blair's Kick Dancers, put on by Brian Epstein's new concert promotion company, NEMS Presentations, in association with the pirate radio station Radio London – followed by her pantomime debut in *Little Red Riding Hood* at Wimbledon Theatre.

Cilla
At the end of 1965 I introduced the Christmas edition of Ready, Steady, Go but I had no ambition at the time to strike out as a TV compère. I didn't think it was my vocation. I thought I'd rather do a musical.

1966

CHATTER ON THE BOX

HIGHLIGHTS

7 JANUARY	**'Love's Just a Broken Heart' released**
13 FEBRUARY	**Top of the bill on Sunday Night at the London Palladium TV show**
25 MARCH	**'Alfie' released**
18 APRIL	**3 week cabaret at the Savoy Hotel, London**
18 APRIL	**Album 'Cilla Sings a Rainbow' released**
3 JUNE	**'Don't Answer Me' released**
11 JUNE	**Special guest star at summer season, ABC Theatre, Blackpool**
6 JULY	**Cilla at the Savoy TV special**
17 JULY	**1st of 4 concert series**
AUGUST	**EP 'Cilla's Hits' released**
14 OCTOBER	**'A Fool Am I' released**
3 NOVEMBER	**West End revue debut, Way Out in Piccadilly, Prince of Wales Theatre**

All through her 1964 Palladium season Cilla had sworn she would ditch her dull hotel-room lifestyle and take a London flat where she would have the freedom to choose her own decor and furnishings. Finally, towards the end of 1965, she got around to renting a cosy little mews cottage five minutes from Regent's Park and fifteen minutes from Piccadilly Circus at a cost of £30 a week. Having somewhere of her own meant that Cilla could entertain showbusiness friends more comfortably.

Cilla

It was a marvellous place but still wasn't home to me. I knew I'd move on somewhere else very soon. I couldn't cook, mind. But I did a great cheese on toast.

Sleeve of 'Cilla Sings a Rainbow' album (UK release). (EMI Records)

Cilla's pantomime debut as a singing and dancing Little Red Riding Hood for the 1965/66 season at Wimbledon Theatre. *(Hulton Deutsch)* (Right) Way Out in Piccadilly, November 1966 to June 1967 – poster.

No fooling: Cilla singing 'A Fool Am I' on Top of the Pops (13 October 1966). 'I used to get my dresses off the peg. It was hard to find short ones which were suitable. It was easier to find nice long ones, which were right for cabaret but not for one-night-stand pop concerts. I liked to be able to move around on stage and jump about a bit with a hand mike and you couldn't do that in a long dress.' *(Rex Features/Barry Peake)* (Right) With Peter Cook and Dudley Moore on their Not Only But Also TV series. *(Syndication International)*

Toothy threesome with plenty to smile about: successful Liverpool stars Jimmy Tarbuck (left), Cilla and Gerry Marsden.
(Rex Features)

Cilla used to phone home from London and speak to her mother almost daily.

Cilla
I tried to persuade my parents to move. Last year in 1965, I offered to buy them a house, but they never wanted to leave Liverpool. I see my parents as often as I can these days – I suppose it averages about once every couple of months. But I never want it to be an occasion when we meet. If I were to visit them and find my mum had made fairy cakes specially, it would spoil everything.

During her 1965-6 panto stint at Wimbledon, Cilla made another appearance on BBC Television's Eamonn Andrews Show, her third booking in little more than six months on what was considered to be the nation's top TV chat show.

This was the series that revealed the second string to Cilla's bow: her gift of the gab in front of a camera coupled with a flair for ad-lib comedy. Theatre and television producers had also noticed her lively and often very funny contributions to panel shows such as Juke Box Jury and were beginning to realise that Cilla had much more to offer in the long term as a TV and stage entertainer than the average pop songstress of the era. It was the versatility which Cilla first displayed on the Eamonn Andrews Show and Juke Box Jury that led indirectly to her emergence towards the end of the sixties as a family television favourite in the role of host/presenter of her own major BBC variety series, and to her eventual establishment as Britains's top ITV personality via the long-running Surprise, Surprise and Blind Date.

Rehearsing for her televised cabaret show, Cilla at the Savoy. (Rex Features)

Cilla's 1966 opened with another hefty hit, the single 'Love's Just A Broken Heart', which she sang when she topped the bill on television's Sunday Night at the London Palladium. As it climbed the charts she celebrated by taking a lightning trip to Paris with her bosom pal Cathy McGowan, a presenter on Ready, Steady Go, ITV's answer to Top of the Pops. 'We'll be too late for the fashion shows but we can always gaze in the shop windows and goggle at all the hairstyles.'

That spring she began to talk more frankly in public about her personal relationship with Bobby. Before then, she claimed, Bobby had been free to go his way on dates and Cilla had gone hers, although neither had formed any other serious partnership. Several papers reported that Cilla was engaged to her road manager and quoted her as saying she hoped to get married the following year.

Cilla

On my dates I found myself thinking increasingly about Bobby. Later I learned I had been in Bobby's thoughts too whenever we spent time apart. It just became quietly accepted between us that we were going steady.

When Cilla released her next single, 'Alfie', *NME*'s Derek Johnson wrote: 'You'll either love or hate this rockaballad.' Burt Bacharach had sent her the song, along with several others, and she ditched plans to record an Italian ballad the moment she heard 'Alfie'. Bacharach came into London to attend her recording session in person.

Cilla

We did fifteen takes, what about that! Usually I only do about four or five. Any one of these with Burt was good enough to release, he really brought out the best in me. 'Alfie' was inspired by the film starring Michael Caine but it was specially written for me by Burt Bacharach. I used to think I was very soulful and sang in an American accent, but if you listen to my early records you'll notice that 'where' and 'there' are two words I couldn't lose my accent on. I thought I had total vocal and accent control on 'Alfie', but I hadn't. I still said 'thur'.

In April Cilla opened in a three-week cabaret season at London's Savoy Hotel. One critic wrote that she captivated a choosy audience 'with a clever mixture of disc successes and

What's it all about? It's Cilla with Burt Bacharach (left) and George Martin at the recording session for 'Alfie'. 'When I first heard Burt Bacharach's 'Alfie' I didn't like the demo disc they played me. I remember on the demo there was a fella singing. Apart from the fact, I mean, you only call dogs 'Alfie'! Also it did remind me of Gracie Fields' song 'Walter'. Besides, you only sang songs like 'Alfie' as a comic record. And I thought, couldn't it have been 'Joshua' or something like that! 'I didn't record it because I thought the film was going to be a hit or anything like that. I wasn't hoping for sales on the basis of the film's success, because the song isn't even in the film. When I recorded the song the film wasn't even out, so nobody knew whether it would be a hit or not.' *(Tony Barrow)*

(Right) 'Alfie' – sheet music. *(Warner Chappell Music)*

(Right) Lending a hand and hoping for a bargain: Cilla and Ready, Steady, Go presenter Cathy McGowan head the queue of helpers as fashionable sixties boutique owner Barbara Hulanicki moves into her new Kensington High Street premises. 'When I get into one of those dresses and put on my eyelashes, I adore being a star. At one time back in the 1960s I'd go out every week to the most expensive boutiques and buy things I'd never even wear. I once bought a £1,000 Paris designer dress I never even had on my back. Eventually I started going shopping with a girl friend, who kept a check on me.' *(Syndication International)*

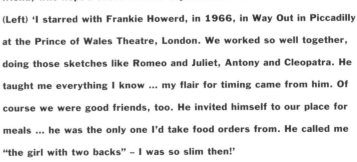

(Left) 'I starred with Frankie Howerd, in 1966, in Way Out in Piccadilly at the Prince of Wales Theatre, London. We worked so well together, doing those sketches like Romeo and Juliet, Antony and Cleopatra. He taught me everything I know ... my flair for timing came from him. Of course we were good friends, too. He invited himself to our place for meals ... he was the only one I'd take food orders from. He called me "the girl with two backs" – I was so slim then!' *(Rex Features/Dezo Hoffmann)*

amusing material geared to a top-class supper room'. Her Savoy act opened with a medley of three standards, 'Misty', 'Tonight' and 'Let There Be Love', and included 'If I Had a Hammer', 'Sing a Rainbow', 'September in the Rain' and 'Big Spender'. On her final Sunday there she starred in her own television special, Cilla at the Savoy, produced by Brian Epstein's newest company, Subafilms. It was the first colour television show of its kind to be made by an independent producer in Britain.

After a short holiday in Portugal, Cilla headed for Blackpool and a sixteen-week summer season at the ABC Theatre, where she appeared as special guest star in Holiday Startime with The Bachelors.

For a performer who had turned professional only three years earlier, Cilla had played a remarkably wide spread of live theatrical engagements on an international scale, from New York's Persian Room and London's Savoy Hotel to holiday shows at the seaside; from concerts at Sydney Stadium to a long season at the London Palladium. Her next challenge was a West End revue at the Prince of Wales Theatre, a production entitled Way Out in Piccadilly, created by the TV comedy script-writing team of Galton and Simpson in collaboration with Eric Sykes. Her co-star was Frankie Howerd, and their stage partnership developed into a close friendship which was destined to last until the veteran comedian's death.

Cilla

On 3 November 1966 I opened in my West End revue debut in Way Out in Piccadilly, the brainchild of the Galton-Simpson-Sykes team and co-starring Frankie Howerd. It was something so new and scary that I told the papers I didn't think I was really cut out for that sort of showbiz after all, but I also admitted I was enjoying it in a masochistic sort of way. In one sketch I had to compare the things of the sixties with those of the twenties. For instance, I took a piece of 'Downtown' and a bit of the oldie 'Sunny Side of the Street', the one that starts: 'Grab your coat and get your hat'. They're songs which are miles apart in time, but the message seemed to be the same.

In a light opera spot I portrayed a geisha girl and Frankie was a rickshaw boy. I sang this a bit like an operatic singer. The others thought I was quite amazing. They were surprised at some of the notes I was reaching. I don't know how I did it – I surprised myself.

The Japanese wig was so heavy it made my hair flat each time I wore it. Consequently I had to wash my hair every night. That year I had the cleanest head in showbusiness.

1967

MANAGING CHANGE

28 MAY	**Top of the bill on Sunday Night at the London Palladium TV show**
JUNE	**EP 'Time for Cilla' released**
2 JUNE	**'What Good Am I?' released**
6 OCTOBER	**1 week cabaret, Variety Club, Batley**
17 NOVEMBER	**'I Only Live to Love You' released**

On Friday 25 August 1967, as he prepared to leave London for a Bank Holiday weekend of partying at his place in Sussex, Brian Epstein received the piece of good news he had been waiting for. Cilla Black was to get her own BBC television series.

Unable to reach Cilla by phone in Portugal, where she had just started a holiday, 'Eppy' dashed off a handwritten note for his secretary: 'Joanne – Please send suitable cable to Cilla requesting she calls me where I am (Sussex or here) a.s.a.p.; I've tried to contact her but impossible. Urgent matter.' By the time Joanne saw the note, her boss was dead.

Brian Epstein died by accident, alone in bed at his Belgravia home, as a result of swallowing a lethal cocktail of booze, prescribed pills and other drugs. Cilla and Bobby were at a nightspot with Tom Jones when a Portuguese waiter broke the news. Cilla felt isolated and desolated by the tragedy. She had never lost anyone so close or attended a funeral before Brian's.

Cilla

Anyone who was really close to him loved him. He was so much more than a manager to me. He was my friend and adviser.

After Brian died in 1967 The Beatles wanted me to come with them to a seance to try to contact him. I didn't go. If he'd shown up I wouldn't have known what to say, and anyway it would only have made his death worse.

Brian Epstein appeared uneasy in the company of most younger women, except for Cilla,

Cilla outside Edinburgh House in Portland Place, where she rented a smart West End flat after giving up her first London home, a mews cottage near Regent's Park. *(Rex Features)*

Making a proper Charlie of herself, Cilla dressed up as Chaplin for The Beatles' Magical Mystery Tour Christmas party at London's Royal Lancaster Hotel. *(Hulton Deutsch)*

(Left) Dig this: for a scene in *Work is a Four-Letter Word* Cilla and David Warner were hoisted over an 18-foot wall in one of the world's biggest mechanical excavaters which weighed 25 tons. 'Filming involved getting up very early but apart from that, it seemed to be the most normal working lifestyle possible in showbusiness. You didn't work weekends. Everything was done for you – they made you up, dressed you, looked after you, fed you. And I loved the tea breaks. The only thing I suffered was the embarrassment. I was supposed to look awful and the way I looked made me self-conscious. I've never liked people gawping at me but I had to get used to it on location shooting. And there were always the technicians staring. In the film studio they had a crew of 90. That's why I could never do a nude scene, not that they asked me to!' *(Hulton Deutsch)*

Cilla with co-stars David Warner and Alfred Marks. 'After completing my film *Work is a Four-Letter Word* in 1967 I became very screen-struck and said that if I could become successful as an actress I'd never sing again. I loved acting, I still do. It's not a bit like making records. It's very frustrating, waiting for a film to be finished and shown – it can take nearly a year – and, where you see the success or failure of a record very quickly, with films you have to wait ages to find out if you were a success or not. That's the hard part. But being a singer is also hard – slogging every night whether you're on one-nighters or in a show. I really thought I'd like to move into films. I decided that if I could act successfully I wouldn't mind if I didn't sing again. The trouble was that my film offers were usually for me to be Gracie Fields or other typical "Northern girl" parts. Me, I wanted to do the heavy stuff, become a Dame and win an Oscar. As a child I read a story in which there was a goose called Dame Priscilla.' *(Hulton Deutsch)*

Way Up In Piccadilly: in Piccadilly Circus, not far from where Cilla was appearing at the Prince of Wales Theatre, her name went up in lights to mark her twenty-fourth birthday. *(Hulton Deutsch)*

whom he adored. He was her greatest fan and he admired her work to the point of obsession, seeing her as the world's next Judy Garland. Whenever they fell out over management affairs, 'Eppy' would be left on the verge of tears, which he held back until she was out of sight. Afterwards he would send her some lavish little gift to make up for their quarrel.

For her part, Cilla was hugely impressed by her manager's sophistication, his immaculate grooming and gentle manner: 'He was everything you wanted a posh fellow to look like, and he had money as well.' At one of their first meetings, he promised to design a whole wardrobe of leather stage outfits for her but his vivid mental pictures never turned into reality.

But for the constant presence of Bobby, Cilla's career might have suffered in the wake of Brian's sudden death. In fact, Bobby and Cilla were already in the habit of discussing all Brian's proposals before she agreed to anything. Consequently, Bobby was thoroughly prepared to slip into the role of personal manager on an official basis when Brian was gone.

1968

IN FRONT OF THE CAMERAS

HIGHLIGHTS

27 JANUARY	*Radio Times* cover and interview
30 JANUARY	1st Cilla TV series begins
9 MARCH	'Step Inside Love' released
6 APRIL	Album 'Sher-oo!' released
22 APRIL	Startime, Alhambra Theatre, Glasgow
6 MAY	Startime, King's Theatre, Edinburgh
6 JUNE	Première of *Work is a Four-Letter Word*, 1st major film role
7 JUNE	'Where is Tomorrow?' released
10 JUNE	1st of 3 cabaret engagements
12 AUGUST	Startime, Opera House, Manchester
26 AUGUST	Startime, Theatre Royal, Newcastle
3 OCTOBER	2nd Australian tour
30 NOVEMBER	Album 'The Best of Cilla Black' released
24 DECEMBER	2nd Cilla TV series begins

The choice of Cilla as David Warner's co-star in director Peter Hall's film *Work is a Four-Letter Word*, a way-out comedy fantasy, came as a surprise to many people in showbusiness. Theatre folk familiar with the strange stage play *Eh?* by Henry Livings, on which the cinema production was based, doubted whether she was suitable to play the part. Others in the light entertainment sector were just as doubtful about the reaction of Cilla's mainstream public to such a weird screenplay, the work of Jeremy Summers.

There was also the view that Brian Epstein had agreed to the project because he was in awe of heavyweight theatrical names such as Peter Hall and Henry Livings, but that he had failed to think it through in realistic terms as a career move for Cilla. *Variety*'s movie critic wrote nothing about Cilla's performance but commented cryptically: 'Director Peter Hall often hangs on to a point just long enough to blunt it.'

As a prelude to the 1968 Eurovision Song Contest, Cliff Richard sang 'A Song for Europe', in special segments of Cilla. Cilla helped Cliff sift through viewers' votes. 'When I had Cliff Richard on my TV show I came out in goose pimples. I couldn't believe it. He was so pretty, still is. He's always been my idol. I remember standing at stage doors all over Britain hoping to see him. Now, here he was, singing on my own show. When he starred at the Talk of the Town in the West End (it's the Hippodrome nowadays), Cathy McGowan and I went to see him. And Cathy sent him a telegram asking him to sing 'Livin' Doll'. Fancy asking for that! But he sang it for both of us.' *(Syndication International)*

(Above) Cilla arriving at the London première of *Work is a Four-Letter Word*. 'When the film *Work is a Four-Letter Word* was released in June 1968 I saw my nose in panoramic VistaVision and I was horrified. It didn't look too bad on a little eighteen-inch black-and-white telly, but up there on the big screen my face looked all nose.' *(Syndication International)*

(Left) Cilla as she appeared in the first programme of her earliest BBC television series in January 1968. *(BBC)*

(Right) 'Step Inside Love' – sheet music. 'I recorded 'Step Inside Love', Paul McCartney's theme of my BBC TV series, and it was released on 9 March 1968. Paul used to write simple songs, but they were difficult to arrange and get the sound you wanted. On the first recording Paul played it on guitar, but the key didn't suit me – and I had to have it taken up. Then the second version was disappointing. I just couldn't get my teeth into it. But we did a great recording in the end.' *(Northern Songs/MCA Music)*

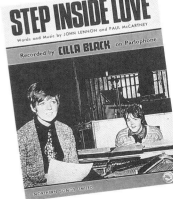

(Left) Sleeve of 'Sher-oo!' album. Cilla's shortest hair style – in length of time it lasted, not actual length of hair – was created by Leslie Russell in 1968 for 'Sher-oo!' album cover photographs which John Kelly took: 'It was a perm that produced a mass of fairly tight little curls. It looked OK for a week and then we changed it. We still laugh about that!' *(EMI Records)*

Radio Times cover, 27 January – at the start of her first television series. (**Radio Times**)

Work is a Four-Letter Word led to other proposals for screen acting roles: 'I've had three or four good offers, and about fifteen lousy ones,' Cilla reported. Eventually Cilla and Bobby wisely turned down the lot in favour of concentrating on television.

Between the end of January and the end of March 1968, the first nine-week prime-time series of Cilla attracted record-splintering BBC viewing figures of over 13 million. The fifty-minute shows featured a spectrum of guest stars ranging from Ringo Starr to Cliff Richard, from Lulu to Sandie Shaw, from Les Dawson to Spike Milligan.

Cilla

When I did my first TV series I'm afraid I put the BBC in an uproar the way I made contact with studio audiences. But I don't see myself playing to millions of viewers. I'm playing to 500 people right there in the studio. So before those shows I used to sing some cheer-up pub songs and try to get a friendly atmosphere going. I like to make friends with the audience and the people on the show. I think that's half the reason the shows were a success. The secret was their length. I could never have done a twenty-five-minute show, I'd have talked too much.

When Ringo Starr made a guest appearance on Cilla, the three other Beatles sent him a telegram: 'Big Brothers are watching and wishing you well. Love from all your Big Brothers!' (*Syndication International*)

Although the massive and immediate success of Cilla the series marked the beginning of a new phase of her professional lifespan as a television entertainer, the show also provided her with another hit record, the programme's theme song, 'Step Inside Love', custom-tailored for the purpose by Paul McCartney but not actually put out as a single until the series was almost over. This was because Paul had written it at the last moment.

In April, Parlophone followed up the single with an

Two great lassies from Lancashire
continued

From the *TV Times* of 2 November 1968 – a feature in which Cilla interviewed Gracie Fields in Capri. 'It was a very exciting time. I got telegrams, not from the Queen, or any royalty at all, but the most treasured telegram that I got on my first night live doing my first TV show was from Gracie Fields. And I still treasure that telegram today.' (*TV Times*)

album, 'Sher-oo!', which as Cilla explained to puzzled journalists was a meaningful Liverpudlian exclamation she'd learned back home in Scotland Road, comparable to London's 'Have a banana'.

In the autumn, Cilla set off on her second tour of Australia.

Cilla

I love Australia. I consider it my second home. I was the first British artist to go there in the sixties and I shook them up with my mini-skirts.

I lost half a stone during my tour Down Under and when I got home I was down to seven and a half stone. Doesn't that sound wonderful! I didn't get a chance to eat a thing in Sydney, I was working so hard. I didn't get time to have more than one meal a day. My first show was at seven in the evening and the second one went on four hours later. I slept too late to have breakfast, so there was just lunch. I had intended to buy all sorts of exotic things, but I brought back a load of rubbish, you know, like those Blackpoolies who buy funny hats with 'Kiss Me Quick' on.

Doing cabaret in Sydney was great. On an earlier trip to Australia in 1965 with Freddie and the Dreamers we flew everywhere and never got a chance to see the places we were visiting. Doing my own cabaret season made all the difference because I was in one place, Sydney, for three weeks. I found Australian audiences much less reserved than British ones. Australians are much more saucy.

1969

WEDDING BELLS

HIGHLIGHTS

25 JANUARY	**Marries Bobby Willis at Marylebone Register Office, London**
7 FEBRUARY	**'Surround Yourself with Sorrow' released**
6 MARCH	**Family wedding, St Mary's Church, Woolton, Liverpool**
20 MARCH	**Spring Show, Coventry Theatre**
19 MAY	**Startime, Alhambra, Glasgow**
23 MAY	**Album 'Surround Yourself with Cilla' released**
27 MAY	**Has nose remodelled**
21 JUNE	**Holiday Startime, ABC Theatre, Blackpool**
27 JUNE	**'Conversations' released**
10 NOVEMBER	**Appears on Royal Variety Show**
18 NOVEMBER	**3rd Cilla TV series begins**
21 NOVEMBER	**'If I Thought You'd Ever Change Your Mind' released**

'Cilla's Wedding
Album' – produced by
Tony Barrow for the
Official Fan Club.

Bobby and Cilla never doubted that they would marry one another, nor did close friends who had watched their relationship develop and mature throughout the sixties. Not only were they very clearly in love, they were also best pals and happy workmates. According to Cilla, the actual proposal was informal to say the least. Bobby said, 'What d'you reckon?' and Cilla replied, 'OK.'

They married in 1969 – twice! The church ceremony which took place in Liverpool on 6 March 1969 was Cilla's second wedding in six weeks. A civil one had been held on Bobby's twenty-seventh birthday, 25 January, at London's Marylebone Register Office. The register office listed the couple as Priscilla White and Robert Willis. 'We didn't want any fuss or hassle, we just wanted to get married quietly,' said Cilla. But newspaper reporters cottoned on at once and cameramen

'When Bobby and I married secretly (or it was supposed to be secret, but the news leaked) at Marylebone Register Office, London on 25 January 1969, Bobby's birthday, I didn't even buy a new dress. I wore a little scarlet mini-dress I'd bought in a Chelsea shop called Granny Takes a Trip. Peter Brown, of the Epstein office, gave me away, the late Tommy Nutter, the tailor, was Bobby's best man and the only other people there were George Martin, my recording manager, his wife Judy, my best friend from Liverpool, Pat Davies, and Gabrielle Crawford, Michael Crawford's wife. I was stupid to think the news wouldn't leak. I did it this way because I didn't want a circus. I thought the Press wouldn't find out, as I'd given my real name at the Register Office, Priscilla Maria White. Of course the Press did find out.' *(Hulton Deutsch)*

Sleeve of 'Surround Yourself with Cilla' album. (EMI Records)

came out in force to cover the occasion. The bride wore a high-waisted scarlet velvet mini-dress which she had bought two years earlier for £8 – she took up the hem to keep it looking fashionable.

Since Bobby was not a Catholic, Cilla had to seek special dispensation: 'Although we were married in law at the register office, we did not become man and wife in the eyes of the church until the later wedding ceremony in March.' The lunch-time wedding in Liverpool was at the picturesque little parish church of St Mary's, Woolton, a few minutes' drive from the home of Cilla's parents. The best man was Bobby's brother, Kenny. Cilla wore long white boots with a short white jersey wool dress trimmed with ostrich feathers, created by the prestigious London fashion house of Jean Varon ('a wedding gift because we're friends'). Bobby was in a grey suit by Nutter's of Savile Row, Tommy Nutter's tailoring firm in which Cilla had a small financial stake.

Only relatives and a handful of the couple's personal friends attended the church. The latter group included the late Brian Epstein's brother, Clive, Cilla's booking agent, Bernie Lee, her recording manager, George Martin, her publicist, Tony Barrow, and fan club secretaries Linda Thomas and Valerie Bettam, who travelled from Birmingham for the

occasion. Cilla bought her own wedding ring, a seven-day luck ring she picked up in Hong Kong on her way to Australia and had altered later to fit.

There was no time for a honeymoon: within a week Cilla was back on telly promoting her latest single, 'Surround Yourself with Sorrow', on Top of the Pops. The record went to Number 3.

Seeing herself so often on television in 1969 made Cilla acutely aware of her broken nose, the result of a childhood

accident which had left a bump just below the bridge and still caused her occasional breathing difficulties. On her birthday in May Cilla booked herself into the Queen Victoria Hospital at East Grinstead, Sussex, for a plastic surgery operation.

Wedding No. 1 – 25 January 1969 in London. *(Hulton Deutsch)*

(Below) 'We tried to keep it underground but the news got out!'

'Although we married in church six weeks later – 6 March – that first wedding will always be, in my heart, *the* one.

'I was brought up a Catholic and Bobby is a Protestant. Still, we did have a Service of Blessing at my mother's local church, St Mary's, in Liverpool. My parents were there and Bobby's family too. I have three brothers – George, John and Allan – and Bobby's brothers are Bertie and Kenny. Dad was able to give me away, my mother wore the lovely hat all brides' mothers wear.

'I wore a cream mini-dress with white boots and ostrich feather which kept getting up my nose and sticking to my lip gloss. My nieces Gina, Lesley and Bobby's niece Jacqueline in scarlet velvet were my bridesmaids. Uncle Jimmy got up at the reception and I thought he was going to make a speech, but instead he sang a song, 'Barefoot Days', and it was great.'

(Peter Brown)

(Left) The knife's for cutting the cake, Cilla! Bobby tries out one of their wedding presents. *(Hulton Deutsch)*

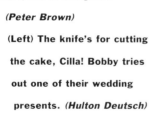

(Right) Wedding No. 2 – 6 March 1969 in Liverpool.
(Hulton Deutsch)
(Left) Cilla with her mother at her wedding at St Mary's Church, Woolton, Liverpool.
(Scope Features)

'If I Thought You'd Ever Change Your Mind' – sheet music. 'I couldn't hide the fact that when I had a flop record I really got depressed. When a single flopped, I felt really bad. You see, one of the things I always used to pride myself on was being able to pick hits. I could just feel it, sort of instinctively. Then I lost the touch when it came to picking hits for myself. Other people – yes. I can still hear someone else's record and tell you whether it stands a chance in the charts.' *(Keith Prowse Music/EMI Music)*

(Above) In the ring at Blackpool Tower Circus for BBC TV's Disney Time. *(BBC)*

(Left) 'I didn't have a badly misshapen nose. Even when I went into showbusiness I did nothing about it. It was Bobby who said I must get my nose seen to. He said it gave me a terrible profile on television. So on my twenty fifth-birthday, of all days, I had it done and of course my secret leaked out.' *(Tony Barrow)*

Cilla with Ginger Rogers at the London Palladium for the 1969 Royal Variety Show. *(Hulton Deutsch)*

(Below) Cilla with TV guest Val Doonican in the third series of her BBC show. 'A lot of people think that 'Liverpool Lullaby' was especially written for me but it wasn't. I was doing a TV show with Val Doonican and he said: "I'm doing a song that is tailor-made for you". It was 'Liverpool Lullaby' and I thought it was lovely, a traditional tune with words by Stan Kelly, and I went into the studio with my musical director. It was one of those magical songs that came off. I always did it on stage because men and women loved it. Some people might think it was a slushy song for mothers who are mad about kids, but it's not. Dads like it too.' *(BBC)*

(Below) 'Conversations' – sheet music. 'I was down at Top of the Pops and the writers Jerry Lordan, Roger Greenaway and Roger Cook were there doing a backing. They said they liked 'Surround' very much and the way I sang it. So I said: "Why don't you write one for me?" – I'd always liked their songs. A little later they sent me five numbers and I recorded them all. Do you know that 'Conversations' is the longest single I've ever done? It lasts for about four minutes. But it doesn't seem that long because it's such a great song and I love it. The late Vicki Brown, who was Joe Brown's wife, was on it and she did a good job. She had a hard vocal sound like Aretha Franklin and she really let herself go on the record. Yet in other ways she was very shy.' *(Dick James Music/Polygram Music)*

Cilla

I felt fine almost immediately after the nose operation, except that I couldn't breathe properly. For a while I felt a bit bashed about and beaten up, but day by day I felt better. Bobby washed my hair one night and that helped. And at the end of the week the plaster was taken off. When the time came I was only too pleased to show off my new nose. It cost me £210. I had a mole removed as well. I was in a private room, so I would not call it outrageously expensive. My nose and teeth made me unhappy and nervous about how I looked, but then I had them both fixed and they looked fine.

I had fractured my nose when I was fourteen. We were in the school playground playing a game called chainy-ayny, swinging each other round. I was on the end of the chain and as we swung round my face went smashing on to the stone of the playground.

Nowadays, knowing I've already had my nose 'done', people suggest that the next thing will be a facelift. I'm waiting till the time comes when the television camera gets too hard on me.

Three weeks after the much-publicised 'nose job', Cilla was back on stage, topping the bill in her own seasonal show, Holiday Startime, at Blackpool's ABC Theatre. Her summer single coupled 'Conversations' and concert favourite 'Liverpool Lullaby', the former written for her by Roger Cook, Roger Greenaway and Jerry Lordan, with orchestral backing supplied by Mike Vickers. The press release from Tony Barrow International read: 'This longer-than-average four-minute performance lets Cilla move between her silk-lined yet soulful balladeering style and the more pungent twistier and shoutier type of delivery at which her voice is equally experienced.'

She rounded off her year with another series of six Cilla television programmes, the first to be shown in colour.

By the end of 1969 Cilla was pregnant.

PART 2

the seventies

....

(Tony Barrow)

1970

MUM'S THE WORD

HIGHLIGHTS

FEBRUARY	**TV shows Amsterdam, Stockholm, Helsinki, Madrid**
14 FEBRUARY	**Named Britain's Top Girl Singer in *Disc and Music Echo* awards**
MARCH	**TV shows Berlin, Paris**
23 MAY	**The Royal TV Gala**
3 JULY	**Album 'Sweet Inspiration' released**
26 JULY	**Robert John born**
4 DECEMBER	**'Child of Mine' released**
22 DECEMBER	***Aladdin* pantomime, London Palladium**
25 DECEMBER	**Hosts Christmas Night with the Stars**

Robert John Willis, first-born son of Cilla and Bobby, came into the world via London's Avenue Clinic on 26 July 1970, weighing 8lb 12oz.

As the proud parents posed for the bedside baby pictures, flowers and telegrams poured in from their families, friends, fans and assorted celebrities. Messages arrived from several of Cilla's 'competitors' – Dusty Springfield, Sandie Shaw and Clodagh Rogers. Ringo Starr and his wife, Maureen, sent a bouquet shaped like a teddy bear.

Cilla's final jobs before the birth included television dates in France and Germany followed by the Royal TV Gala, a starry spectacular recorded in the presence of the Queen and shown by the BBC ten days later, on 23 May.

The press claimed the pregnancy cost Cilla £100,000 – the fees they reckoned she would have earned from the television, concert and cabaret appearances, including tour dates abroad, that had to be cancelled. Cilla told them: 'Having a baby is more important than all the money in the world.'

(Right) Cilla and Bobby leaving the Avenue Clinic in St John's Wood after the birth of Robert John. 'When I had Robert I had planned to take six months off work but after four weeks I was going mental. It was when I found myself hoovering the carpets in my sequined frocks that I knew it was time to go out to work again. I think if I didn't work I'd just about shrivel up.'

(Hulton Deutsch)

While they waited for Robert John to arrive, Cilla and Bobby went house-hunting. They had already exchanged the Regent's Park mews cottage for a larger London flat situated opposite Broadcasting House in Portland Place but, as Cilla said at the time, 'I can't bring a baby into this flat, plus a nanny and two dogs.' It wasn't as if they went in for miniature or even regular-sized breeds of dog – their choice was a pair of very large and very friendly Briards, a type of French sheepdog, called Sophie and Ada.

(Scope Features/David Magnus)

The dilemma was to find a permanent home base large enough to raise a family, close enough to town for Cilla to keep her television, recording and other appointments without wasting too much time travelling, yet far enough from central London's noisiness, polluted atmosphere and congested streets. Having their first child convinced Cilla and Bobby that the time had come to seek more peaceful surroundings and to relieve some of the stress and tension caused by

their hectic urban lifestyle.

Weeks after Robert John's birth, by which time things were getting a bit desperate, they went to view a place close to Denham Golf Club in rural Buckinghamshire. The gardener's house, a red-brick building in the grounds, looked so large that Cilla thought it was what they had come to see.

(Right) An album that never was: Cilla walked Briards Sophie and Ada near her London flat and the press reported she was plugging her next album which would be called 'Cilla 'n' Sophie 'n' Ada'. Nearly right, it was called 'Images'. (Syndication International)

Cilla said she might well have taken the red-brick 'cottage' to the side of the front drive, not out of desperation but because it looked so inviting. Set in almost seventeen acres of landscaped garden and lawns, woodland and a green meadow, the eight-bedroomed main house proved irresistible: 'When we looked over it, we were like a couple of kids. Every room was wonderful.'

Journalists have questioned Cilla repeatedly over the years about her recipe for a happy marriage. She makes no secret of the fact that private and professional sectors of her life are kept apart. When she is Ms Cilla Black, Bobby takes charge of her business affairs and deals with the bookers, producers and agents.

Cilla

We never row about business. Bobby's responsibility is to manage that side. It is up to me to respect his judgement over the jobs I do – and the ones he decides it's better not to do.

But when she is Mrs Bobby Willis it's another story. Cilla turns her back on stardom to become an entirely different woman. She might be a million miles from the entertainment world when she concentrates on being a wife to Bobby and a mother to Robert John, Ben and Jack. Travelling so much together as a working team before they married gave Cilla and Bobby ample opportunity to iron out their differences and exhaust most sources of disagreement.

Cilla with another of her all-time favourites, Bob Hope, on Christmas Night with the Stars, December 1970. *(BBC)*

Cilla

We taught ourselves to accept one another's failings at a time when most engaged couples knew next to nothing about their partners. The birth of a baby changed our outlook. Prior to 1970 most of our energy went into my

Below: (Left) One of her teenage Hollywood idols, Jerry Lewis, was a guest during the fourth series of the Cilla show. *(BBC)*
(Centre) 'Go on, have a guess at the title of my pantomime at the Palladium this Christmas!' *(Associated Newspapers Group Ltd)*
(Right) Cilla and Ringo go all Mexican for her BBC-TV series. *(BBC)*

career. Now we started to consider the wants of this new little person.

That Christmas I couldn't go back to Liverpool as I was doing the London Palladium panto. It was the first time I hadn't spent Christmas in Liverpool with my family, as I had only Christmas Day off and had to be back in the theatre next day to do two shows.

It was snowing that Christmas Day. Bobby and I were alone in our dirty great eight-bedroomed house in Denham where we'd recently moved and our nanny had gone home to Wales. I phoned my mother to wish her happy Christmas and she said 'How's Robert?' I told her I'd put him out in the garden, where he'd been asleep for three hours and he was fine. Mother said 'Put the phone down and bring him in immediately.' I hadn't realised, as a new mother, that cold makes babies sleep. Though he was well wrapped up, he could have died of hypothermia. And I thought I was so careful; even when Robert had a spot on his cheek I'd called out the paediatrician.

At London's Café Royal on 14 February for *Disc and Music Echo*'s 1970 Valentine Awards, Cilla collected the title Top British Female Singer and was given a trophy to prove it. Other winners included Cliff Richard and Lulu. *(Hulton Deutsch)*

1971

TWO ROBERTS

HIGHLIGHTS

	Voted Britain's Favourite Girl Singer of the Year by *NME* readers
	Voted Personality Mother of the Year by *Confectionery News*
23 JANUARY	**4th Cilla TV series begins**
MAY	**Album 'Images' released**
11 JULY	**6 concert tour**
24 SEPTEMBER	**3rd concert tour of Australia**
7 OCTOBER	**2nd concert tour of New Zealand**
6 NOVEMBER	**5th Cilla TV series begins**
15 NOVEMBER	**'Something Tells Me' released (later awarded Silver Disc)**
25 DECEMBER	***Aladdin* pantomime on television**

When Robert John was fourteen months old, Cilla and Bobby flew to Australia and New Zealand for concerts which had been cancelled the previous year when she was pregnant. While Cilla did the postponed dates, the infant Robert was sent off on a holiday of his own with his nanny:

Cilla

We had to be Down Under for several weeks so we fixed this little jaunt for Robert, a cruise round Greece, something we'd never done ourselves, because we didn't want him to feel lonely! I think the real reason was to clear our own consciences. We were the only ones left feeling lonely, we missed him like mad.

Asked to name various favourite things in 1971, Cilla said the view she looked forward to most each morning was 'My two Roberts: the smaller one

A fifth series of Cilla, including five 'live' shows, was broadcast in November and December 1971. *(London Features International)*

(Left) In the dining room at Denham: Robert John's first birthday party. 'In a lot of ways I'll follow my parents' example as regards religion, we'll let Robert John choose for himself as he grows up. But Bobby and I agree that the important thing is for our son to be a good Christian, irrespective of what denomination he adopts.' *(Scope Features)*

(Far left) Sleeve of 'Images' album. *(EMI Music)*

wide awake and peeping over his cot rails, the much larger one I married still fast asleep.'

After a two-year absence from the Top Ten, Cilla crashed back into the pop charts in 1971 with 'Something Tells Me (Something's Gonna Happen Tonight)', penned by Roger Cook and Roger Greenaway as the new signature tune for her latest Cilla television series. It rose as high as Number 3 and stayed among the best-sellers longer than anything since 'You're My World'.

(Above) Cilla and Bobby with something to celebrate at the *Sun* newspaper's TV Awards — readers voted her their Top Television Personality for the second year in succession. *(Sun)*

(Right) 'We're trying hard not to spoil Robert John. I can't stand precocious children, I was one myself, a proper show-off, I must have been to go into showbusiness.'

(Hatton Features Syndication Ltd)

(Above left) Big-hearted *Confectionery News* came up with a new award for Cilla in 1971 and made her their Personality Mother Of The Year. *(Keystone Press Agency c/o Hulton Deutsch)*

(Above right) 'My Liverpool strip show!' Striking shot of Cilla with Liverpool soccer boss Bill Shankly at the team's practice ground. 'If it was up to Bobby, Bill Shankly would have been made Prime Minister.' *(Syndication International)*

(Left) Stars of the Beeb's 1971 Christmas panto, *Aladdin*, recorded at Wimbledon Theatre: surrounding Cilla are Alfred Marks, Norman Vaughan and Roy Castle. *(BBC)*

1972

I DO LIKE TO BE BESIDE THE SEASIDE

HIGHLIGHTS

	Voted Top Female Vocalist by *NME* and *Disc and Musical Echo* readers
	Voted Top TV Personality by *Sun* readers
6 FEBRUARY	**1st of 3 cabaret engagements**
11 FEBRUARY	**'The World I Wish For You' released**
23 APRIL	**1st of 3 concert dates**
28 JUNE	**International Spectacular '72, the Opera House, Blackpool**
17 NOVEMBER	**'You, You, You' released**
25 DECEMBER	**Christmas Night with the Stars**
30 DECEMBER	**6th Cilla TV series begins**

In 1972 Cilla's twin successes as pop singer and TV star were running parallel and she received public recognition in the form of poll awards in the two sectors of her career. On the one hand, record fans who read the *NME* and *Disc and Music Echo* voted her Top Female Vocalist . Meanwhile, readers of the *Sun* newspaper made her Top Television Personality for the third consecutive year. Booked to star for six summer weeks in International Spectacular '72 at Blackpool Opera House, Cilla broke box-office records at the venue and the run of the show was extended by twelve weeks to a total of eighteen, one of the resort's longest-ever seasons.

Cilla

When I first started interviewing people for the telly, hardly anybody recognised me. After all, who would expect Cilla Black to turn up on the front at Clacton in the middle of winter? I think it's my voice that people recognise first. There have been times

Cilla with Ronnie Corbett on Christmas Night with the Stars *(BBC)*

Mother and son doing well: Robert John was growing up fast. 'Being a mum is the most marvellous thing. There's nothing in the world, not a gold record or an audience that applauds forever, that can match that feeling. I suppose the big difference about being a parent is that it makes you less selfish.'
(Below right) *TV Times* cover – 25 March 1972. (*TV Times*)

when I've been wearing sunglasses, or I've been muffled up against the rain and cold, and people have still known it's me the moment I started to talk.

Rumours circulated among fans in the summer of 1972 that Cilla was about to bring out a recording of a song written for her and produced by former Beatles guitarist George Harrison, with Ringo Starr playing drums. The story was based on truth, as most rumours are. One Sunday during her summer season in Blackpool, Cilla travelled to London on her day off to record George's composition, 'I'll Still Love You'.

Cilla
The words were super but I'd been to the dentist that morning and all my mouth was swollen. I wasn't in the mood to record and it was a very hot Sunday and the session didn't come off. I tried it again, with Dave Mackay producing, but even then it didn't have the magic that it deserved. It should have had a 'Yesterday'-type arrangement.

Although millions saw Cilla on the BBC's Christmas Night with the Stars, she spent the holiday at home with her family, having pre-recorded the television show a fortnight beforehand. Cilla's mother came down to Denham for the festivities and Frankie Howerd was invited to Christmas lunch. 'My mother's going to fall in love with Frankie and Robert's just old enough to know what's going on and to take an interest in a family Christmas.' She said the catering plans were all worked out: 'Bobby takes charge of the turkey, I'll be the vegetable cook and also look after the pud.'

1973

PARTY TIME

HIGHLIGHTS

JANUARY	**Album 'Day by Day' released**
APRIL	**Concert tour of South Africa**
MAY	**Named Top Female TV Personality in *Sun* TV awards**
20 MAY	**1st of 12 concert dates**
13 SEPTEMBER	**The Cilla Black Show, London Palladium**
20 OCTOBER	**'Gold disc' presented by EMI Records to mark 10 years with the company**

Cilla admitted that her New Year wish for 1973 was to have a second baby: 'I'm not preggers yet, it just hasn't worked out, but we'd like to have a baby this year.'

Her sixth series of live Cilla shows for the BBC contained the usual mix of musical and comedy guests plus innovations. Viewers were invited to suggest dreams they would most like to come true: 'We had some outrageous suggestions. What some women wanted to do to Engelbert and Tom Jones is no one's business!'

Cilla and Cliff Richard – *Radio Times* cover 13 January 1973.

(Radio Times)

Before the series was transmitted, Cilla recorded an experimental half-hour situation comedy with actors John McKelvey, Sam Kelly and Avis Bunnage, who played Cilla's mother. This extended the idea of including comedy sketches as part of the show's format and it went out as a special segment of a Cilla programme at the beginning of February. Nothing specific was said at the time, but Cilla's associates were well aware that she was ambitious to act in a full-blown situation comedy series of her own and was using the existing Cilla show to test the water.

Voted Top Female TV Personality by readers of the *Sun* for the fourth year running, Cilla celebrated her tenth anniversary in showbusiness in several ways. She did almost a dozen one-night-

(Right) 'He didn't take off too much, did he?' After her latest visit to see her hairdresser, Leslie at Smile, Cilla checks her new-look shortened hairstyle for 1973. 'Ten years ago I was still working in an office and I couldn't have guessed what was going to happen – that I'd be a singer and have my own TV show. So how can I say where I will be in another ten years? I'll be pushing forty in ten years' time and if I'm still working then in 1983 I want our Robert to be proud of me. I hope I'll grow old gracefully like Elizabeth Taylor, I don't ever want to be thought of as mutton dressed as lamb.' (Sun)

(Below right) Cilla makes it four in a row as she accepts her latest Top Female TV Personality trophy from Rolf Harris at the Sun newspaper's 1973 Awards. (Sun)

The Cilla Black Show at the London Palladium: backstage with Roger Whittaker and the famous Tiller Girls dance troupe.

(Syndication International)

stand concerts, mostly at weekends in large seaside theatres, a couple of nights (four shows) in cabaret at Batley's famous Variety Club in Yorkshire and a seven-week twice-nightly season at the London Palladium. Entitled The Cilla Black Show, the lavish £100,000 Palladium production was directed by veteran Dickie Hurran, the man responsible for staging some of Britain's most spectacular shows during the heyday of modern variety.

Sleeve of 'Day By Day' album.

(EMI Records)

Previewing the show, London journalist James Green wrote: 'She's a kind of northern Bisto Kid who gets a great deal of pleasure out of singing and doesn't give a thought to nerves on the big occasion, lucky girl!' Cilla recalled her first Palladium season nine years earlier: 'Do you remember that awful beehive hairdo? I could hardly walk straight it was so heavy but I thought it was gear at the time.'

The most extraordinary gig of Cilla's anniversary year, perhaps of her entire thirty-year career as an entertainer, took the form of a fan club get-together held at a West End disco, Tiffany's in Shaftesbury Avenue, one Saturday that October.

Positive response to the invitations sent out was so great that the event was divided into two 'houses', the first at 11.00 a.m., the second at 2.00 p.m., so that a total of well over 1,200 club members from all over the country could attend. As they arrived at each session, members were handed souvenirs including an anniversary mug, a brochure and a colour portrait. EMI Records boss Gerry Oord presented Cilla with a commemorative 'gold disc'

LONDON PALLADIUM SOUVENIR BROCHURE

London Palladium Souvenir Programme September/October 1973. 'Sometimes my son thinks I'm crackers over my stage dresses. He's been seeing me walking around at breakfast time in this incredible black gown I wear at the Palladium. But I've got to feel happy in a stage dress, and I can't until I've got used to wearing it at home.'

Trendy Savile Row tailor Tommy Nutter, a personal friend of Cilla and Bobby, made her a stunning white satin-trimmed suit for the opening of her eight-week autumn season at the London Palladium. The Cilla Black Show marked the entertainer's tenth anniversary in showbusiness.
(Syndication International)

plaque. Cilla met members in person, signing autographs endlessly throughout the whole shindig. Cilla joked: 'A few minutes ago I had to hold this man's briefcase while he searched for a pen. I bet he wouldn't have made me do that if I'd been Shirley Bassey!' Finally, to wind up each session, Cilla put her personal commentary to a short 'home movie' she had made at Denham for the occasion. By now the Willis family's seventeen acres of Buckinghamshire were being shared with ten Briards and some horses.

Cilla

My mother has been living on her own since my dad died, yet every time she stays here at Denham, she can't wait to get back to Liverpool where the action is. She's very much a town lady.

Before 1973 ended, Bobby was able to make a proud announcement to the press: 'Cilla expects our second baby at the beginning of next May.'

1974

ENTER BEN

HIGHLIGHTS

4 JANUARY	**'Baby We Can't Go Wrong' released**
5 JANUARY	**7th Cilla TV series begins**
30 APRIL	**Benjamin born**
17 MAY	**Named Female TV Personality of the Year in the *Sun* TV awards**
24 MAY	**'I'll Have to Say I Love You in a Song' released**
7 JUNE	**Album 'In My Life' released**
12 AUGUST	**Holiday Startime, Futurist Theatre, Scarborough**
5 OCTOBER	**1st of 3 concert dates**
25 OCTOBER	**'He Was a Writer' released**
27 OCTOBER	**Gala concert, London Palladium**
26 DECEMBER	**Boxing Day BBC TV special**

Cilla kicked off 1974 with a new single, her first in more than twelve months, and a new recording deal. Following the termination of her long association with George Martin, Bobby negotiated a fresh five-year recording contract for Cilla with EMI. At new sessions which took place just before Christmas 1973 a total of four new recordings were produced independently by David Mackay, who had worked with Cliff Richard and the New Seekers among others.

Until the last moment there was no plan to change the theme of her Saturday evening BBC television series, still 'Something Tells Me', but the A-side of the latest single, 'Baby We Can't Go Wrong', turned out to be so strong that everyone concerned voted to make it Cilla's new signature tune to open and close each programme.

Baby Ben makes his debut: his first pictures were taken by David Magnus at Hammersmith's Queen Charlotte's Hospital. 'I won't be buying anything new for this baby because I still have all of Robert's things. I've asked all my relatives not to give me baby clothes. But I hope this one likes my singing a bit more than Robert does, it's Gary Glitter he enjoys.' *(Scope Features/David Magnus)*

(Left) Holiday Startime, Futurist Theatre August to September 1974 – brochure and handbill.

Cilla

A long time ago I gave up predicting hits but I do know 'Baby We Can't Go Wrong' is my personal favourite from the first four titles I recorded with Dave Mackay, a bit different from anything I've done before.

However, despite weekly plugs on her own show and a shoal of other TV spots, including Top of the Pops, 'Baby We Can't Go Wrong' was not one of her biggest hits, rising no higher than the mid-thirties in the Top Forty, her last pop chart entry to date.

Over the next few weeks, Cilla went back into the studio to stockpile tracks for another album, eventually released in June.

Announcing Cilla's new nine-week TV series, producer Colin Charman, who died tragically later the same year, named Bernard Cribbins and Twiggy as the first guests: 'We wanted to get away from the regular run of variety guests, inviting instead actors and more unusual people.' A comedy sketch in the initial programme featured Bernard Cribbins and Cilla as young club leaders in the bridal suite of a seaside hotel. After finishing this seventh series of programmes Cilla took a rest during her last months of pregnancy.

(Tony Barrow)

The baby, a second boy they named Benjamin, was born on 30 April, weighing 7lb 11oz, at Queen Charlotte's Maternity Hospital in Hammersmith, London. When Liverpool won the Cup final the following Saturday, Bobby said: 'I knew we would complete the double, it's been a wonderful week.' Cilla added, 'I couldn't be more delighted about both events.' To help lose the few extra pounds she had put on as a result of the pregnancy, Cilla joined Bobby on the golf course ('We live opposite so I try to get out there when the weather's nice').

At the end of May, while Cilla and Bobby were holidaying in Spain with Jimmy and Pauline Tarbuck, news broke at home of a motorway scheme which threatened the part of

Denham where the Willis house was located. SINGER CILLA BLACK AND ACTOR ROGER MOORE COULD LOSE THEIR £100,000 COUNTRY HOUSES, screamed one national newspaper headline. The scheme was for the part of the new M25 linking the M4 and M1, and in the end one of several other alternative routes was chosen and the Willis and Moore properties remained unaffected.

In July came the announcement that Cilla would be doing a situation comedy series for ITV but she hastened to confirm that this was not the end of her relationship with the Beeb:

'I've seen you on our telly!' Cilla collects the views of a cooperative young fan for the Beeb's 1974 August Bank Holiday Special broadcast from Brighton. *(BBC)*

'That would be like a child turning on her own mother.' Cilla said she was keen to have a go at an acting series but was worried about sticking to her lines for the sake of the professional actors who would surround her: 'I'm an ad-libber, good at making things up on the spur of the moment, but I'll try very hard to keep to the script.'

1975

CASA ROLL

HIGHLIGHTS

15 JANUARY	**Cilla's Comedy Six TV series begins**
21 FEBRUARY	**4th concert tour of Australia and 3rd tour of New Zealand**
28 MARCH	**'Alfie Darling' released**
19 MAY	**Named Britain's Top Female Comedy Star by the Writers' Guild**
16 JUNE	**Summer season, Congress Theatre, Eastbourne**
20 JULY	**1st of 2 concert dates**
25 JULY	**'I'll Take a Tango' released**
11 SEPTEMBER	**Concerts at King's Theatre, Glasgow**
25 SEPTEMBER	**Birthday Show, Coventry Theatre**
29 NOVEMBER	**1st of 5 concert dates**

Great happiness and dreadful grief combined to make 1975 a bitter-sweet year for Cilla and Bobby. Professionally speaking, Cilla broke new ground in January with the first of half a dozen situation comedy shows for ATV. Personally, she and Bobby were heartbroken in October by the death of their third baby.

On 4 October, during the run of an autumn stage show at Coventry Theatre, Cilla gave birth to a baby girl. She lived for half a morning, from dawn to breakfast time. Solely for the purpose of putting something down on paper for the authorities, Cilla and Bobby named her Helen. They deliberately selected a name they didn't feel strongly about, and one which had not been on the little list they had drawn up during the pregnancy. After a fortnight's bed rest ordered by her doctors, Cilla resumed work and went back to her Coventry season but the production's title, Birthday Show, now had a cruel

Proof that true stars can't resist dressing up even when they haven't a show to do! To the left of Cilla and Bobby is Jimmy Tarbuck who threw this fancy dress 'do' in London for showbiz pals to celebrate his birthday. Guests included Bruce Forsyth and Anthea Redfern, Bobby Moore and Peter Gordeno. *(David Magnus)*

(Left) Cilla, Bobby and Ben help Robert to celebrate his fifth birthday. 'Robert likes babies. He doesn't squeeze them too hard like other boys. I suppose it's because he likes animals.' *(Scope Features/David Magnus)*

ring to it. She was unable to talk about Helen for half a year afterwards, and then only with tears held back.

Much later, she was persuaded by Birthright, a charity for research into abnormalities in childbirth, to talk openly about the tragedy.

Cilla

My baby daughter lived for only two hours and I can never, ever forget that. One day everything was fine, I was feeling marvellous and looking forward to the baby being born. Next day my life was shattered, my little girl was dead, and all I could think was 'Why me?'

At the Pye Ladies Of Television luncheon at Grosvenor House, London, on 19 May 1975, Cilla was named Britain's Top Female Comedy Star, chosen by judges appointed by the Writers' Guild Of Great Britain. Previous winners of the title, actresses Polly James (left) and Nerys Hughes congratulated Cilla. *(Hulton Deutsch)*

For the first time in six years, Cilla did not win one of the *Sun* newspaper's 1975 TV poll awards, largely because there was no Top Female Personality section. On the other hand she did win another quite different 1975 award when the Writers' Guild Of Great Britain named her Britain's Top Female Comedy Star at the Pye Ladies of Television luncheon in May. This came in the wake of Cilla's Comedy Six, her first-ever series of comedy plays, written by Ronnie Taylor and produced by ATV.

With two growing youngsters to consider at holiday times, Cilla and Bobby decided to look for their own villa in Spain, having stayed at hotels or friends' places in Spain and Portugal for many years.

They found what they were looking for on a hillside facing the sea on the coast between Marbella and Estepona, a piece of land large enough to take a small whitewashed *casa*, a decent-sized garden and a kids' swimming pool. Naturally there was a golf course attached to the development to provide for Bobby's basic vacational needs.

Cilla

I blame it all on Jimmy Tarbuck. I'd never fancied Spain until I went over to see his little villa there. I love the sun but Bobby hates it and sits in the shade on the terrace when he's not playing a round of golf.

Being a fresh development, the property was known at first only as 'Plot 3' – until Robert came up with Casa Roll. The Willis family still pays regular visits to the place, particularly after each new series of Blind Date and Surprise, Surprise is finished. What began as a three-bedroomed villa has been extended to cope with visiting relatives who join Bobby, Cilla and the boys in Spain from time to time. Nearby lies the vast Atalaya Park hotel and resort complex and a little way along the road Marbella's millionaires' marina Puerto Banus with its smart quayside shops and seafood restaurants. Although they keep a short-list of favourite places to dine out, Cilla stocks the villa's fridge from the supermarket when they arrive.

Cilla

The British are the only people who frown upon children when they walk into restaurants. In Spain, it's smashing, the Spaniards dote on children. Even so, I still take 5lb of bacon with me from Denham, and sometimes minced beef or frozen hamburgers. They think I'm crackers at Heathrow Airport.

1976

CILLA AT THE PALACE

HIGHLIGHTS

11 JANUARY	**1st of 3 cabaret engagements**
14 FEBRUARY	**8th Cilla TV series begins**
12 MARCH	**'Little Things Mean a Lot' released**
MARCH	**Album 'It Makes Me Feel Good' released**
9 AUGUST	**Summer season, Congress Theatre, Eastbourne**
31 AUGUST	**Cilla's World of Comedy TV series begins**
SEPTEMBER	**'Easy in Your Company' released**
10 NOVEMBER	**Cilla at the Palace, revue, Victoria Palace, London**

Cilla's 1975 set of half-hour comedy plays for ATV had notched up such healthy viewing figures that the series was constantly among the top three shows of the week. The ITV company went ahead with six more the following year and the result was that Cilla found herself with a 1976 series on both BBC and ITV.

To coincide with her eighth Cilla series, she made a new EMI single, reviving a golden oldie for the first time in her twelve-year recording career. She chose 'Little Things Mean a Lot', a Number 1 hit for American songstress Kitty Kallen way back in 1954: 'Since the song is twenty-two years old there will be a whole generation of record buyers who won't have heard it before. In any case my arranger-producer Dave Mackay has made some big changes in the interpretation.'

She introduced the new single for the first time on her BBC show on 13 March. Also issued that month by EMI was Cilla's latest album, 'It Makes Me Feel Good', which included tracks produced at her first recording sessions in American studios, a venture linked to the US chart entry of her single 'I'll Take a Tango', in the late autumn of 1975.

On 5 May, less than three weeks after the last programme of the current Cilla show was aired, she began recording her second series of six situation comedies for ATV under a new title, Cilla's World of Comedy. These were broadcast between the end of August and the

Cilla faces the camera for a *TV Times* front-cover shot.

(Scope Features)

Slim hoofers stepping out: Cilla and Marti Caine were presented with Schweppes Slimline Awards at the Inn On The Park Hotel, London, two days before Cilla's thirty-third birthday. 'I weighed just eight stone on my thirty-third birthday in 1976. If I could attribute my shape to anything other than "just nature" it must be hard work and nervous tension which kept my weight down. I didn't have any personal problems, my love life and family life were always happy and I could eat plates and plates of chip butties without putting on an ounce. If I'd known then, seventeen years ago, that a time would come when I'd be constantly striving to keep my weight down I'd have started sooner on eating the right foods to keep slim.' *(Hulton Deutsch)*

'By 1976 I was on my eighth BBC TV series of Cilla, and the first show took a hammering from the critics. It was no surprise. I had never been the television critics' darling. This time they all attacked at once on the first episode. In fact it turned out to be my most successful series in the eight years I'd been doing them

SOUVENIR BROCHURE

and the ratings were very good. After the critics had slammed it, I had a telegram from Paul and Linda McCartney who I hadn't seen in ages. "Don't listen to the critics, gel," they said, "We think it's a smashing show." This kind of thing reassured me that I wasn't losing my touch.

'Perhaps the interviews with the public in that particular series didn't work out so well. But chattering to strangers comes naturally to me. I do it all the time. And because of my shows strangers have always felt they could be very personal with me, which I don't mind either. One evening at a night spot a girl I didn't know came up to Bobby and me and said, "I think it's wonderful that you two are still together." I agreed with her! I think I've been very lucky in my private life.' *(BBC)*

(Left) Cilla at The Palace – souvenir brochure.

Cilla with actor Richard Wilson in Desirable Property, one of the Cilla's World Of Comedy episodes recorded in May 1976. (Tony Barrow)

first week of October and used as their theme song Cilla's September single 'Easy in Your Company'.

This was one of Cilla's busiest years since the height of her pop star era in the mid-sixties. Apart from the wealth of television appearances, she fitted in two major stage shows, first a summer production running for almost two months at Eastbourne's Congress Theatre, and secondly an American-influenced revue, which opened at London's Victoria Palace in November.

It was ten years almost to the week since Cilla had been in a West End revue – Way Out in

Piccadilly with Frankie Howerd in 1966. Her 1976 co-star in *Cilla at the Palace* was another close pal, Jimmy Tarbuck. The new show had a couple of heavyweight US showbusiness names behind it – producer Alan Lee, who cast Hollywood stars for Broadway productions and had worked with a host of top headliners in Las Vegas, and his partner on a total of sixteen American productions, choreographer Jerry Jackson, who had worked with star 'hoofers' such as Juliet Prowse, Goldie Hawn and Abbe Lane.

Jackson's creative approach to Cilla's £200,000 show at Victoria Palace lay somewhere between the Folies Bergère of Paris and the Sahara Hotel of Las Vegas. Even the specially refurnished backstage quarters for the stars were relatively luxurious by West End theatre standards.

Cilla

Your average estate agent would have called my dressing-room a luxury flatlet – with noisy neighbours, but handy for theatre-goers. I was on the move all the time, slipping in and out of different costumes. I even had one complete change of outfit which happened onstage in the middle of a dance sequence.

One of the many special effects had Cilla singing 'Fool on the Hill' while three larger-than-life images of herself on giant screens provided pre-filmed vocal accompaniment. Cilla also sang 'Keeping Young and Beautiful', wearing a little blonde wig.

The *Sunday Mirror* called it 'a bright, lively show with no-expense-spared costumes', while the *Daily Telegraph* talked of 'warm-hearted personalities in a bobby-dazzler of a show', adding that care had been taken and money had been spent to make this something more than the usual noisy spree. The *Daily Express* observed that 'this kind of entertainment has a romantic heritage and jaded palates were sharpened again.'

America's entertainment industry bible, *Variety*, called the show a 'Las Vegas-style spectacular' with 'the glitter, gimmicks, costumes and effects associated with Parisian nightlife … the sort of lavish extravaganza uncommon in Britain.'

Cilla at the Palace ran successfully for six months. The entertainer's only regret was that the producer's much-published intention to take the production, including both Cilla and Jimmy, to America after its West End stint failed to materialise, partly because, as *Variety* noted at the time, 'though household names in the UK, top-liners Tarbuck and Black are virtually unknown in America'.

1977

BYE BYE BEEB

HIGHLIGHTS

30 MAY	**1st of 8 cabaret engagements**
19 JUNE	**1st of 7 concert dates**
15 JULY	**'I Wanted to Call it Off' released**
25 OCTOBER	**Cabaret, Kuala Lumpur, Malaysia**
27 OCTOBER	**Cabaret, Singapore**
31 OCTOBER	**Concert tour of New Zealand**
10 NOVEMBER	**Cabaret, Australia**
NOVEMBER	**Voice-over for Cadbury's TV commercial**

The invitation came indirectly from high places. The Rt Hon. Lord Shawcross wrote to Lord Delfont: 'Dear Bernie, As I think you know, we have been granted time on Independent Television for the Birthright Appeal on behalf of the Royal College of Obstetricians and Gynaecologists by Granada. They have suggested that Cilla Black should be asked to do it. I understand she is under contract to you…'

Dickie Hurran, theatrical producer for the Bernard Delfont Organisation, wrote to Cilla's publicist: 'I spoke to Cilla this morning and it appears that she had been approached by her own gynaecologist to make such an appeal and had in principle agreed to do so.'

Thus, on New Year's Day 1977 in an ITV appeal for Birthright, Cilla lent her name to a worthy cause which was particularly close to her heart, and one with which she continued to be involved:

Cilla

I frequently get asked to appeal for charities because I am Cilla Black, but this time it was also because I was personally involved. I am one of the women Birthright could help. I know what it is like to have a baby who dies. It is a shattering experience that we hope one day no woman will have to go through. The one question that nobody had been able to answer for me, not even the top gynaecologists, was why our baby daughter had died in 1975. So I realised how important research into this subject was.

'Sitting at my piano the other day.' In October 1977, Thames Television dragged a piano onto the pavement outside their Euston Road studios to provide an off-beat photo opportunity when Cilla had been signed up to make a one-hour Spectacular. In the background are Philip Jones and Iris Frederick of Thames Television. This was not the first meeting between Cilla and Philip as she made one of her early television appearances on Thank Your Lucky Stars in 1963 singing her first single 'Love of the Loved', when Philip was an up-and-coming producer. 'With Thames I get six weeks to do one show, which means they have to be perfect. It's a lot different from the BBC shows which were done live.' *(Thames Television)*

Prior to 1977, the winning over of Cilla, a BBC regular, by ITV bosses had been restricted to situation comedy and had not affected her annual series of variety shows on the Beeb. Now the big guns of commercial television came out and Thames announced that she was joining ITV: 'Cilla Black has been wooed over from the opposition for an undisclosed sum and is to make a one-hour spectacular for Thames Television next spring.' Behind the 'courtship' and the irresistible deal which followed it was light entertainment controller Philip Jones, who had worked with Cilla fourteen years earlier when she sang 'Love of the Loved' on Thank Your Lucky Stars and he was an up-and-coming young producer at ABC Television.

Cilla introduced her only single of 1977, 'I Wanted to Call it Off', produced by Mike Hurst and arranged by Colin Frechter, on BBC Television's Seaside Special in July. Her other numbers on the show were Paul McCartney's 'Silly Love Songs' and a contemporary Gladys Knight hit, 'Baby Don't Change Your Mind'.

Without a lengthy TV series to prepare and record, Cilla took a holiday in Spain with Bobby and the boys when her revue at the Victoria Palace closed. But the fortnight's break was cut short so that they'd be home in time for Bobby to see the 1977 Cup final at Wembley.

1978

PRINCESS CILLA

HIGHLIGHTS

14 APRIL	**1st of 2 cabaret engagements**
12 MAY	**'Silly Boy' released**
18 MAY	**1st of 3 concert dates**
24 MAY	**Thames Television TV special**
16 JUNE	**The Cilla Black Show, summer season, Princess Theatre, Torquay**
JUNE	**Album 'Modern Priscilla' released**
22 SEPTEMBER	**'The Other Woman' released**
22 DECEMBER	***Dick Whittington* pantomime, Empire Theatre, Liverpool**

Writing about Cilla's first UK concert of 1978, at the Capitol Theatre, Aberdeen, in May, critic Kenny Gordon commented in the *People's Journal*: 'I thoroughly enjoyed the Cilla Black Show last Thursday – much to my amazement. Cilla's kind of music is not what normally appeals to me, but on the whole I found the concert most entertaining.'

The rest of the review was typical of the press notices Cilla's stage shows received in the seventies. Cilla had stopped making chart hits so critics didn't feel they should describe her as a pop singer. On television she had been trying her hand at comedy acting and she was hosting 'specials', although she no longer had her own weekly variety series. Consequently, critics were not sure what to expect. Kenny Gordon wrote: 'Cilla came onstage with an advantage over most acts. While most stars have to work to build up an empathy with the audience, Cilla had it right there without even trying. For so long, through live performances and even more so, through television appearances, she has come across as a warm and friendly character, and it was only natural that the audience would expect the same in her show here. They got it.'

Cilla with Frankie Howerd at the recording of her first Thames TV Special in March 1978. *(Scope Features)*
(Left) The Cilla Black Show, Princess Theatre, Torquay, June to September 1978 – souvenir brochure. 'To
succeed, you have to keep your face in front of people. I could not retire now and expect to come back at
forty. You have to grow alongside your audience.'

Cilla

I'm not a distant legend to be admired from afar as, say, you admire a star like Sir John Gielgud. My fans feel really close to me. One fella the other night got so excited he actually pinched my bum – and me a married woman of thirty-five.

Cilla's trick was to use her flair for audience communication and her singing talent in equal measure during a stage show. Her fifty-minute act was half musical and half one-woman chat show. She did all the old hits, including 'Anyone Who Had a Heart' and 'Step Inside', plus recent releases such as 'Nobody Does it Better' and 'Silly Boy', but she also involved her concert audiences in comedy participation sequences centred, for example, around 'If I Had a Hammer'. As Kenny Gordon concluded: 'The show was enjoyable enough to merit three encores, and when Cilla finally left the stage there were smiles on the faces of every person there.'

For the second year running Cilla was seen on television in a commercial for Cadbury's Dairy Milk chocolate, the first product she had ever advertised. The firm's marketing director, Gareth Hughes, commented: 'Cilla is absolutely the right person to do the ad. She has a congruence with the brand. It is universally popular and she has a very high degree of popularity. She can portray enjoyment easily and Dairy Milk is about enjoyment.' Quite so.

In March Cilla recorded what was intended to be the first of several 1978 TV specials for Thames. In one sequence Cilla was done up as a punk rock guitarist accompanying Frankie Howerd; in another she partnered Ricky May in a sing-along duet. Unfortunately, industrial action at the Teddington studios of Thames Television caused the cancellation of the remaining two shows in the planned series which should have been recorded in the autumn after Cilla's summer season at Torquay.

On 25 November 1978, Bobby Willis announced the launching of his new Mayfair-based artists' management company, Hindworth, with former NEMS Enterprises booking agent John Ashby as his managing director. Bobby told the press: 'Although we have expansion plans, particularly in the area of production, we will be offering a highly personal service to each individual act on our client roster.' In addition to Cilla, Hindworth's initial list of acts included Los Amigos Paraguayos, Malcolm Roberts and Julie Rogers.

Relaxing but still in the active management mode, Bobby plugs Cilla's Torquay summer show via the T-shirt he just happened to be wearing when a *Daily Express* photographer called. That's Ben beside Cilla and Robert on the far right. *(Daily Express/Peter Shirley)*

(Above left) Sleeve of 'Modern Priscilla' album. 'In fifteen years I never did a TV commercial until the one for Cadbury's because I was afraid of over exposure. But lately I took eighteen months off TV to concentrate on my new LP so I was pleased to do the chocolate ad.' *(EMI Records)*

(Left) 'I'm very slow to make friends, I'm very suspicious, I weigh people up like mad but I can't alter. We have a lot of acquaintances, but we can count on the fingers of one hand the people we can ring up and say: "Hello, what are you doing?" Real friends are people you don't have to get the best silver out for. You can eat in jeans and sweaters in the kitchen. Actually, we do that all the time, or from our knees in front of the telly.' *(Daily Express/Peter Shirley)*

1979

ROOTS

HIGHLIGHTS

MAY	**TV shows, Madrid**
MARCH	**Cabaret tour of Australia**
9 JUNE	**Summer season, Winter Gardens, Bournemouth**
21 DECEMBER	***Aladdin* pantomime, Wimbledon Theatre, London**

At the end of 1978, Cilla returned home to Liverpool for the pantomime season at the Empire Theatre, Lime Street, her first appearance as Dick Whittington. Cilla spoke nostalgically about her own childhood visits to Christmas panto.

Cilla

The whole of our street went every year on Boxing Day, but we could never afford the Empire; we were taken to the old Shakespeare Theatre nearby and we always sat high up in the 'gods'.

In the eyes of Merseysiders, particularly struggling local performers, the prestigious Empire ranked as a sort of London Palladium of the north. This was where a youthful Cilla had queued up twenty-two years earlier to see her favourite American singing group, Frankie Lymon and the Teenagers, and where The Beatles once had failed to make their mark in a talent contest.

Apart from a couple of BBC television appearances, Cilla's 1979 was devoted to stage work, with longer gaps between dates so that she could spend more time at home in Denham with

Happy family: Cilla with Bobby, Robert and Ben at home in Denham. *(Daily Star)*

(Left) *Aladdin*, Wimbledon Theatre – handbill. 'I had two specials set up and one Christmas show but they were cancelled because of the ITV strike. I couldn't make up the lost time afterwards because I was playing *Aladdin* in pantomime at Wimbledon. Still, it doesn't matter too much because Janet Brown did me on Mike Yarwood's show. Our Robert saw it and said it was marvellous, just like me.'

Robert and Ben. In the spring she returned to Australia for major concert and cabaret bookings and in the summer she starred for sixteen weeks at Bournemouth Winter Gardens. For Christmas, it was panto again, *Aladdin* at Wimbledon Theatre.

For *Aladdin*, Cilla had her hair cropped quite short because she was playing the title role.

Cilla

No problem for me to play a fella because I've got the right chest for it already. Robert took one look and told me I looked a bit punkish. He quite likes having a punk mum.

'Whenever Bobby goes out to play golf I miss him and I'm on the phone to the golf club within a few hours. I know it sounds soppy but I can't help it.'
(Reveille Newspapers Ltd)

PART 3

the eighties

1980

AND JACK MAKES THREE

HIGHLIGHTS

25 FEBRUARY	**7th concert tour of Australia**
MARCH	**Concerts in Kuala Lumpur and Bangkok**
29 JUNE	**1st of 10 concert dates**
3 AUGUST	**Album 'Especially for You' released**
20 OCTOBER	**Jack born**
23 NOVEMBER	**1st of 2 cabaret engagements**
DECEMBER	**11 concert tour of the Middle East**

During her 1980 tour of Australia and the Far East, Cilla discovered she was going to have another baby.

After losing their only daughter, baby Helen, only hours after her birth, Cilla and Bobby waited a couple of years – on doctor's advice – before starting to try again, initially without success. She became rather paranoid and frustrated, but only those in her closest family circle knew how she was feeling.

Cilla

I got myself ever so healthy, but nothing happened. When it did, I just thought wow, I'm pregnant! It came as a total surprise because I had given up hope of another child. I love being pregnant. I'm never healthier than when I'm expecting. It's hard to keep it secret because I look so good.

In May, five months before the new baby was due, Cilla said she'd like a third son.

Cilla

In the past I'd wanted a girl, but then I thought I'd like another boy. I'd become used to having men around the house. I had a scan and I saw the baby on the screen. I was convinced it was a boy, although everyone laughed at me when I told them.

Bobby brings Robert and Ben to meet newly
born Jack at Queen Charlotte's Hospital in
October 1980. *(Scope Features)*

Cilla had already decided to take a break from summer season in 1980, opting for one-off concerts at seaside resorts instead. In view of her good news, she decided to take things as easy as possible, cancelling an autumn season at Nottingham's Theatre Royal and shelving plans to make a TV pilot. 'It was for a brand new television idea but the doctor advised me not to do it – I don't want to take any chances.' Cilla gave birth to a baby boy, Jack, on the morning of 20 October in Queen Charlotte's. It was said to be a very easy and quick birth with no problems. The Willis family as it is today was now complete.

Meanwhile, her latest sixteen-track album, 'Especially for You', on the K-Tel label, earned a Silver Disc by selling an impressive 60,000 copies in its first couple of months in the shops. When the album was advertised on TV with a series of commercials partly filmed at home in Denham, some sharp-eyed fans noticed that the sleeve they saw was not the one in their local shops. The commercial was prepared before K-Tel and Cilla had agreed on the sleeve's final design and a prototype was used for the cameras and then discarded. Recorded in May and June and produced by Bruce Welch, 'Especially For You' contained a wide spread of different styles, from Mike Batt's 'Bright Eyes' to The Bee Gees' 'How Deep is Your Love'; from the *Evita* hit 'Don't Cry for Me Argentina' to Billy Joel's 'Just the Way You Are'.

This was also the year that saw the inauguration and 'official' recognition of Cilla's Circle of Fans, organised by Joan Organ, Sarah and Sue Evans, Donald Holgate and Alan Hardy to replace the London-based fan club of the sixties and seventies which had closed down. Cilla had one sad piece of news to give fans that summer: elderly Briards Walter and Sophie had had to be put to sleep because of chronic illness. The good news was that Ada, Dingle and Leo were still very much alive and kicking and had been joined by a 'new baby' Briard bitch, Hazel, born in February.

Behind the scenes in 1980, discussions were already taking place for an important new TV series. Cilla knew that negotiations were far from complete but she couldn't resist dropping the first hints about the show, indicating that if it went ahead at all it would be made by one of the independent (commercial) companies. She admitted that most of the suggestions being put to her for television were based on variations of the variety-style format which she had done for the BBC for nine years.

Cilla

I wanted a different format. At the latest talks about a new series I found it was the first time in eighteen months I'd got excited about an idea. I know the BBC made me what I am today, but I don't think they could have afforded this kind of programme.

(Left) Concerts at Fort Regent Gloucester Hall, St Helier, Jersey – poster.
(Right) Cilla's publicity shot at the opening of the eighties. 'I know performers who are physically sick before they go on, but not me. Once I get into the sequined dress, you can't hold me back.' *(Tony Barrow)*

1981

THE NATURAL RED-HEAD

HIGHLIGHTS

28 JANUARY	**1st of 6 cabaret engagements**
6 FEBRUARY	**1st of 24 concert dates**
MAY	**8th concert tour of Australia**
15 JUNE	**Summer season, Festival Theatre, Paignton**
9 DECEMBER	**London Night Out TV show**

woman

o2's greatest weekly for women

january 31 1981 20p

After the heartache...
WHY JACK IS
SPECIAL TO CILLA

Wear it anywhere!
Super sweater dress-
just £11·95

BAD BACK?
Don't take it
lying down

DALLAS: can
the new boy
beat J.R.?

FREE
INSIDE!

Be first to read
DANIELLE STEEL'S
passionate
new novel
THE RING

Young Jack Willis celebrated his first birthday slightly early. But the fact that Cilla and Bobby brought out the single-candled cake before the proper date didn't seem to bother him in the least.

He seemed equally underwelmed when Mum and Dad flew off on holiday to Morocco twenty-four hours before his real birthday. Maybe Jack sensed as he waved them off from behind his baby-walker that he was being left in caring hands: Cilla and Bobby had the same nanny, Penny, to look after all their three boys as they grew up and she is still a well-loved and virtually indispensable part of the Willis household today.

Unlike his pair of fair-headed brothers, the last addition to the family had red hair. People told Cilla Jack's hair would surely darken during the first year but she watched and saw no change.

Cilla

I nearly died when I saw this vivid red hair. I rang my mum in Liverpool and she couldn't understand it either because we're not known for red-heads in the White family, and Bobby couldn't have been blonder. All the dye I used on my hair over the years must have

Dressed to sing: Cilla concentrated on a full diary of concert and cabaret dates in 1981. *(Daily Express)* (Far left) *Woman* cover — 31 January 1981. *(Woman)*

got into my bloodstream! When he got older, Jack kept threatening to dye his hair another colour.

Helen, the baby daughter we lost, would have been fourteen months younger than Ben. To carry a baby, to give birth, and then to lose it is awful. You blame yourself. You feel total guilt all the time. You take comfort by saying it wasn't meant to be, because

Jack's first birthday was brought forward twenty-four hours so that Bobby and Cilla could celebrate with their family before leaving for Morocco.

the baby's lungs just weren't properly formed, but it's such a shock. Jack was the new baby I wanted for so long but he was no replacement or substitute for our Helen, nor ever intended to be. There was a time after losing the baby when I thought I'd never be able to sing 'Liverpool Lullaby' again. At the beginning Ben found the arrival of a new baby a bit strange. We had

to be careful with him; Ben had been my baby until then and suddenly after an enormous gap there was our Jack; Ben began saying things like 'Why are you kissing him all the time?' and I knew it was only half in fun.

In 1981 Ben joined Robert at his 'big school', Thorpe House at Gerrards Cross, where the poet Sir John Betjeman used to be a master. Robert was preparing for his 11-plus exams: 'We'd like him to go to Merchant Taylors' School afterwards but we know how hard it is to get in there,' said Cilla.

Cilla
If I'd had more chance of a good education myself I could have been a brain surgeon,

because I was a very bright child. With children, you've got to give them their heads. You can't keep them under Mother's wraps forever. It's just that in this society now we don't have the feeling of community we used to have. We don't have the habit of looking out for other people's children. When I was a child our door was never locked. You never had to lock up because there was always someone around to keep an eye on your house.

Being a working mum isn't so unusual these days as when I started having children. Today there isn't much money about so a lot more mothers have jobs. It's the rule rather than the exception. I feel less of a freak than I used to.

When Russell Harty hosted a special Christmas edition of his BBC chat show in his own home at Settle, Yorkshire, renowned hotelier/restaurateur John Tovey prepared the turkey for guests Cilla and (far right) Madge Hindle. *(BBC)*

As the year closed, Cilla declared: 'There's no pressure on a showbiz marriage if you're successful. When couples break up, just look at the success sheet. When the theatre's empty that's where the pressure is.' Bobby added: 'Married life isn't The Dick Van Dyke Show but we love each other so the relationship is worth working at twenty-four hours a day.'

Cilla

Before my appearance on ITV's London Night Out, hosted by Tom O'Connor, I'd been away from show business for much of that year as I wanted to spend more time with my family. So I made a point of watching myself – a thing I rarely do. Why? I couldn't believe the show was actually going on. First the recording was cancelled because of an ITV dispute. At the second attempt there was a bomb scare and we had to clear the studio and adjourn to a pub. On the third attempt we succeeded. But my brother phoned from Liverpool, right in the middle, to say our Mum had fallen and broken her hip. I was about to sing 'It's a Miracle' – and I reckon it was a miracle the show went out!

1982

BOBBY'S GIRL

HIGHLIGHTS

17 JANUARY	**1st of 17 concert dates**
25 JANUARY	**3 concerts, National Concert Hall, Dublin**
18 JULY	**Concert series, North Pier, Blackpool**
2 AUGUST	**6 concerts at the Adam Smith Centre, Kirkcaldy, Scotland**
23 AUGUST	**Concert series, Grand Theatre, Swansea**
29 OCTOBER	**9th concert tour of Australia**

Cilla

I could never ever do a show without Bobby. Only twice in eighteen years have I had to manage without him. A lot of people forget what managers do. Bobby's not lurking about all the time, he's not always with me nowadays. What he does is more of an office job, he's got to do all those nasty things which I don't hear about like haggling over money and generally planning my career.

In one of his very rare interviews, Bobby revealed that he had found the problem of 'role reversal' within their relationship a tough problem to tackle in earlier days: 'The biggest difficulty was adjusting to a situation where the woman in my life would earn so much more than I could. Then it started sinking in that there was a real need for me to be around. I realised how dependent Cilla was. I was not just protecting her as a bodyguard might, but carrying out specific jobs like the lighting and sound at concerts.'

During the second half of the seventies, Bobby had beefed up his own earnings by opening Hindworth, a London management agency and concert promotion company which developed into a thriving business concern. But he recalled how it had been in the sixties: 'If I started out with an inferiority complex or a sense of jealousy because Cilla was becoming a big star, I lost all that during our early years away from Liverpool. Money stopped being a problem between us when I began to make quite a bit from writing the B-sides on Cilla's hit singles.'

Family portrait by David Magnus, one of Cilla's most prolific photographers during the first twenty years of her career. 'Our Robert was built like a brick toilet. He was captain of the rugby team. I used to lie about my age to our Ben, but I decided I'd tell him the truth when I was forty. When our Jack was beginning to fill out a bit he loved a fight after his bath and packed quite a punch even at two-and-a-half.' (*Scope Features/David Magnus*)

Bobby also looked back on the days leading up to his wedding to Cilla: 'I cannot remember a specific time when I stopped thinking about Cilla as just another girlfriend and started considering her seriously as the future mother of my babies. We never thought seriously about marriage in advance. It happened so fast all our friends were amazed.'

Cilla was seventeen when she met Bobby, three years before she turned fully professional as a singer and made her first record.

Cilla

I hadn't even heard of the pill until I was at least eighteen but the big thing was to be warned that you'd throw your life away if you went and got yourself 'into trouble'. I do remember girls at school in Liverpool becoming pregnant – it was not uncommon – but I remember promising myself at the age of fourteen that it would never happen to me. Bobby and I shared the view that getting married at any age was pointless unless the couple concerned were planning to have children. In the sixties, we chose to delay any thought of a wedding date until we were ready to think about a legitimate pregnancy.

1983

TWENTY YEARS ON

HIGHLIGHTS

17 JANUARY	**Album 'The Very Best of Cilla Black' released**
22 JANUARY	**Appears on Wogan**
2 FEBRUARY	**1st of 2 cabaret engagements**
9 FEBRUARY	**TV shows, Holland**
20 FEBRUARY	**Top of the television bill in Live From Her Majesty's, Her Majesty's Theatre, London**
28 FEBRUARY	**1st of 31 concert dates**
5 MAY	**Appears on Top of the Pops, 1,000th edition**
17 MAY	**Pilot TV show for Surprise, Surprise**
SUMMER	**Typhoo Tea TV commercial**
1 AUGUST	**Summer season, Pier Theatre, Sandown, Isle of Wight**
19 DECEMBER	***Jack and the Beanstalk* pantomime, Hippodrome, Birmingham**
24 DECEMBER	**Cilla Black's Christmas Eve TV show**

Cilla opened her twentieth year in the business with a hugely entertaining TV appearance on the Wogan chat show, followed by an equally well-received bill-topping spot on Live From Her Majesty's, which included seven of her most popular songs. Despite these outstanding TV dates, showing the best of both sides of Cilla, the question most frequently fired at the entertainer by her fans in 1983 was: 'Why don't we see more of you on the telly?' She said: 'I tell them I haven't dropped out and I wouldn't dream of retiring. I enjoy my work, I have no plans to shut up the shop.'

The truth is that Cilla was on television at least twenty times during 1983, but her fans wanted her back in a full-blown weekly programme of her own and she admitted that good new programme ideas with a musical theme were hard to

find. She added that if she ever took on another television series of her own, it would need to be something particularly challenging.

Cilla

I am bored to tears when I see a singer on television do nothing more than stand there and go through a set of songs. I'd rather put on the album, I'd rather just listen to records than watch that. I wouldn't have done a series in the eighties unless I'd thought it was going to be better than my original Cilla shows for the BBC. The strength of those shows was that we used loads of fresh ideas which were all new to television.

Champagne signing: outside LWT's South Bank headquarters Cilla celebrates the signature of her contract to host Surprise, Surprise, heralding the beginning of another extraordinarily successful phase of her lengthy television career. 'There are still lots of singers and groups from the old days going around but people think they've vanished because they don't see them on the box. I've still got lots of my original fans and I've got new ones too – all thanks to television. It's got nothing to do with the records you make. When you appear on TV, it makes or breaks you.' *(Rex Features)* (Far left) *Weekend* cover – 5 October 1983. 'On my fortieth birthday in May 1983 Frankie Howerd bought me a special cake without candles. He said he was going to wheel it in with one for every year of my life, but was beaten back by the heat.'

Sleeve of 'The Very Best of Cilla Black' album. (EMI Records)

One other factor played its part in making Cilla cautious and selective over new television work: the loss of her scriptwriter, Ronnie Taylor.

Cilla

When Ronnie died, it was like losing my right arm. Ronnie had written everything I ever said on television, all the sitcoms, the sketches, the links. Whatever channel I appeared on, it was Ronnie who gave me all my words.

At one point in 1983, Cilla thought she might have found an attractive new television format, although she never looked upon it as a long-term proposition. It involved three thirty-minute programmes produced by Bryan Izzard for Channel 4 under the working title of The Green Tie on the Tail of the Little Yellow Dog. When she was first approached by the producer who wanted her to do Gracie Fields monologues, Cilla told him she didn't do impressions, Janet Brown was the one he should talk to. Izzard explained that she would be acting out 'Walter, Walter Lead Me to the Altar', but not imitating Gracie's voice.

Along with other assorted artists ranging from Julie Walters and Leonard Rossiter to Arthur Askey and Ronald Lacey, Cilla would play a guest at a dinner party where everyone would do a party piece. Cilla took part in two of the programmes.

Cilla

We filmed over two days in a wonderful old house in London's Bloomsbury, a music museum in Brunswick Square. They were shown in the summer of 1983 and that was as far as the project went.

Meanwhile, on 17 May, between the planning and the transmission of the Channel 4 programmes and ten days before her fortieth birthday, Cilla recorded a pilot show for Surprise, Surprise. Alan Boyd, London Weekend Television's head of light entertainment at the time, said that the strength of the proposed series would lie in Cilla's magical touch with the audience: 'When we made the ninety-five-minute pilot that came through very clearly.'

Cilla could well sing in the series but this would not be a staple ingredient, said Boyd. Phone-ins might be included and there would be recurring items each week to build up audience loyalty. Although anchored in the studio, there would be substantial outside recording throughout the country.

Revealing that he had been working on the idea for a long time and had modified it after a decision had been taken to produce it with Cilla as the star, Alan Boyd described Surprise, Surprise as 'one of ITV's major new entertainment ventures in the coming year.' Boyd added that LWT was thinking in terms of sixty-minute slots for Surprise, Surprise: 'A one-hour show is a lot for a single presenter to sustain, though, which is why we have brought in Christopher Biggins as a "mate", to be a roving reporter, as it were.'

Writing in an October newsletter to Cilla's Circle of Fans, Joan Organ summed up the fans' delight at the events of 1983: 'She made a triumphant return to the charts with a compilation album of her hit singles, gave viewers of the Terry Wogan chat show the biggest laugh they'd had for a long time and earned herself a three-year contract with London Weekend Television as host of a new series of programmes involving the public. Cilla can now look forward confidently to have even more successes to her credit by 1988, her silver anniversary.' Circle members contributed to several twentieth-anniversary gifts for Cilla, including a cheque for Birthright, a Silver Disc, a set of crystal champagne glasses and a carriage clock, and Cilla put in a personal appearance at Circle celebrations in October to cut the massive birthday cake.

One person, *Sunday People* columnist Nina Myskow, joined in Cilla's twentieth anniversary celebrations in her own ingenious

Summer Season, Sandown Pavilion, Isle of Wight, August 1983 – programme. 'When I was appearing in Sandown during the summer of 1983, a little girl in the audience said to her mother in a rather loud voice: "Mum,

when is she going to sing that 'dirty song'?". Heads turned and people started to laugh! I realised that the song she was referring to was 'Liverpool Lullaby'. She had remembered the lyrics, "Oh! you are a mucky kid."'

way, by voting the entertainer Wally of the Week: 'Cilla Black, who with one wavery swoop of her voice wiped out her wonderful appearance on Wogan the other week, is this week's wally. Her warbling as the star turn on Live From Her Majesty's last Sunday was woeful. Wally of the Week. Cilla dear, it's not that I don't have a heart. Anyone who had an ear – never mind two as I have – must have wondered what it was all about. You never did have much of a voice. But the remains have floated straight down the Mersey. Stick to your mad-as-a-hatter lovely chatter. Remember, Miss Black, it's best never to go back.'

Cilla

If people criticise my work – well, I'm getting a bit long in the tooth to be annoyed. I learned at an early age that if you can't stand the heat you should get out of the kitchen.

Cilla closed the year in panto, *Jack and the Beanstalk*, at Birmingham. Ann FitzGerald reviewed it in the *Stage* newspaper: 'Cilla Black is the Jack with the awkward task of killing an invisible giant, but by then she's built up such a marvellous rapport with the children in the audience that they are happily persuaded by anything she does.'

When Cilla asked the Birmingham kids how she should kill the invisible giant, one young Nina Myskow fan yelled back, 'Sing to him!'

Before Surprise, Surprise went into production, Cilla made a Christmas Eve special for LWT to kick off her exclusive contract with the ITV company. Guests

An anachronistic traffic bollard made a convenient prop when Cilla did a pre-opening photo call for *Jack and the Beanstalk* at Birmingham Hippodrome.
(Right) To mark her twentieth anniversary, Cilla's Circle of Fans presented her with a commemorative Disc when her latest concert tour came to Lewisham Odeon on 15 October 1983. (*Sarah Evans*)

included Frankie Howerd, The Bee Gees and Julio Iglesias, who appeared by satellite to sing a transatlantic duet with Cilla. There was also a dream sequence in which Cilla played Ginger Rogers, Judy Garland, Carmen Miranda and Gracie Fields ('I loved doing Judy Garland because it gave me a chance to flash my legs').

Cilla

It was great to have Frankie Howerd on my ITV show Cilla Black's Christmas Eve. I wanted somebody stable and solid in case anything went wrong. Mind you, I made a right fool of myself with Julio Iglesias. I tried out my Spanish on him and he couldn't understand a word I was saying.

During breaks in the recording of Cilla Black's Christmas Eve, Cilla and Bobby waited near a dressing-room phone for a call from Robert, who was expecting to get his exam results.

Cilla

Thank goodness Robert phoned as soon as he got the result, and he had passed. We were very proud of him. He had achieved so much more than Bobby and I ever did with our education. It really made my Christmas. I let him have his BMX bike early!

I'm glad we have been able to give our children an expensive education although they had to earn their pocket money doing odd jobs. I feel a bit bitter about my own lack of education. Jack had a terrible time with his dyslexia until we found out what the problem was. He wouldn't read any books and he had trouble with his spelling. He was getting frustrated and so was I. But once he'd been labelled a moderate dyslexic he came on in leaps and bounds. He thinks it's wonderful. It's like he's special, so he doesn't have a hang-up about it any more.

Where I came from – Scotland Road, Liverpool – there were so many of us kids that we had forty-eight pupils in my class at school and we never got the attention we needed. I was very lucky, though, that I got a place at a commercial college, and the chance to train as a secretary.

1984

A NEW VENTURE

HIGHLIGHTS

6 MAY	**Surprise, Surprise TV series begins**
16 JULY	**Summer season, Royalty Theatre, Great Yarmouth**
12 AUGUST	**1st of 5 concert dates**
14 OCTOBER	**2nd Surprise, Surprise TV series begins**
26 DECEMBER	***Dick Whittington* pantomime, Apollo Theatre, Oxford**

In March 1984, refreshed after her post-panto holiday in the Virgin Isles, Cilla prepared for the launch of Surprise, Surprise by going out and about on location to film items for the initial series of programmes. Originally planned by LWT as a Saturday-night series, the first episode was eventually shown on Sunday 6 May and (no surprise, no surprise) met with mixed reactions from the press. But even Sarah Evans from Cilla's Circle of Fans was unsure at first, as she told members in their next newsletter: 'I must confess that when I went to the recording of the first Surprise, Surprise show I was not over-enthusiastic about the format, but once the edited version was transmitted my opinion changed.'

Sarah continued: 'As the series progressed with Cilla and co-presenter Christopher Biggins settled in and became more relaxed, the shows were highly entertaining. The highlights were the various filmed reports where Cilla revealed herself as a bit of a daredevil, what with being the subject of an air-sea rescue, going up in a Lancaster bomber, visiting an oil rig, driving a train and cleaning an alligator's teeth.'

Cilla

In May 1984 on Surprise, Surprise I had to crawl through the narrow entrance to the alligator pen at a zoo in Poole, Dorset, with express orders to clean the alligator's teeth. I assumed the zoo staff had given the alligators an injection to keep them quiet. They said they had turned the heating off for twenty-four hours and that this would make the alligators hibernate. But the camera crew had their lights on for hours in advance and it had warmed the beasts up again.

The Good Old Days? A music hall sequence from the third series of Surprise, Surprise. 'I've gone from being the girl next door to the auntie next door. Soon, I suppose, I'll be the granny next door! I try to look glamorous, but the trouble is everything falls apart as soon as I open my gob. If fans saw Shirley Bassey in the street they'd kiss her feet. But they treat me like one of the family.' *(London Weekend Television)*

The idea was that the alligators need their teeth cleaned twice a week and I had to do the necessary. Well, I had this toothbrush about eighteen inches long and I stuck it out at this thing that looked like a handbag. It lunged forward and snapped the toothbrush handle right off. I came within inches of losing my arm. I wasn't worried about that so much as the fact that I had on a very expensive diamond ring.

I scrambled out of that pen like a bat out of hell. I discovered later that they didn't even have a gun handy in case anything went wrong – and they'd insured me for a fortune. I'm very gullible. I believe anything anybody tells me.

The last three of the six shows were broadcast 'live', the first of them on Cilla's birthday, with Surprise, Surprise guest Frankie Howerd providing the cake. It was generally agreed that the 'live' element boosted the adrenalin among both cast and production crew so that the atmosphere in the studio each weekend became charged with a very special excitement. It was rather like working without a safety net, just as it had been for Cilla in her earliest days at the BBC, when she used to say that she felt at her best when shows were going out live and there was a sense of great urgency, danger and adventure about each week's programme.

TV Times cover, first series of Surprise, Surprise, 5 May 1984.

(TV Times)

Cilla

On Surprise, Surprise I planned to sing 'Rescue Me' to gallantry medal-winner John Hodder, helmsman of the Lyme Regis inshore lifeboat. While doing this I was to be in a fishing boat apparently drifting helplessly off the Dorset coast.

The sea was so rough I was yearning to be rescued for real. The wind blew my false eyelashes off. It was no joke, I can tell you. The boat was rocking so violently the sound engineer went more green than me and the cameraman had to tie his hat on with string. It was terrifying. I thought the boat was going to roll over. And on shore the cameraman had to be lashed to the harbour wall.

I was so grateful when the lifeboat lads rescued me. They just threw me into the lifeboat. Doing a stunt like that showed how trusting I was and it didn't put me off. I've even gone up in a hot air balloon, although I hate flying and get a nosebleed if I stand at the top of the stairs.

As for the harsh words of the newspaper critics, Cilla said simply: 'I've been in this business too long now to let those things get me down.' Significantly, the good ratings proved how little the public cared about what the critics had to say. At the end of the day it was the viewers who mattered.

Cilla

Believe it or not I quite enjoy the criticism I get for Surprise, Surprise, Wally of the Week and so forth. I would have taken offence twenty years ago, but if I met these critics at a function today I wouldn't be bitter. What would upset me is if they thought that I was a load of rubbish but felt they couldn't say so, perhaps because they'd met me and we'd got on well or something like that.

I only get upset about bad reviews or distorted stories in the papers when it affects members of my family. My mother used to ring me up, so I had to go through the rigmarole of telling her they only knock success. I had to do a public relations job with my family.

There were other reasons why this became a time of trauma and unhappiness for Cilla in the midst of her joy at seeing viewing figures soar.

A few days before her birthday, during rehearsals for the first live edition of *Surprise, Surprise*, there was more dramatic news as Cilla was taken into hospital at short notice. CILLA BEATS OP TO KEEP A TV DATE cried the *News of the World* the following weekend. 'Plucky Cilla Black will appear live on TV tonight just twenty-four hours after leaving hospital following emergency surgery after haemorrhaging at her mansion home in Denham, Bucks.

'She was given a blood transfusion and taken to the operating theatre. But the courageous star mum asked to be patched up temporarily so that she could appear on ITV's *Surprise, Surprise* show.'

Three weeks later, Cilla cancelled four nights in cabaret at Blazers, Windsor, and went into St George's Hospital, Tooting: 'It's nothing sinister, just a woman's complaint.' On 15 June she had a hysterectomy. The operation was a total success and Cilla sent a message to her fans: 'I'm alive and kicking and I'm still smiling!

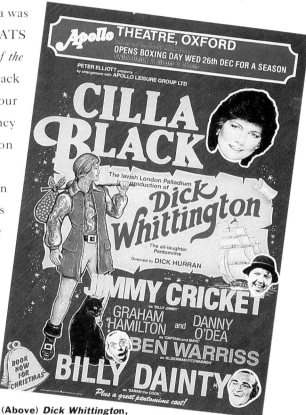

(Above) *Dick Whittington*, **Apollo Theatre, Oxford, December 1984 – handbill.**

I can't wait to be up there on stage.' On 16 July she opened her summer season at Great Yarmouth's Royalty Theatre on schedule, doing nine shows a week for eight weeks.

London Weekend Television announced that they were so pleased with *Surprise, Surprise* that a second extended series of nine shows would go out in the autumn. In effect this secured Cilla's future as a top ITV presenter.

Surprise, Surprise

As Cilla and Christopher Biggins settled in and were more relaxed, Surprise, Surprise became highly entertaining. 'On Surprise, Surprise I have to psych myself up to keep in control during the reunions. Otherwise the show would fall to pieces with all of us weeping. Whenever I'm near tears I think of my Mum and that pulls me together. I remember years ago crying at the end of my first TV series. The audience was crying and so was the floor manager. Afterwards my Mum gave me an awful earful, for showing her up in front of millions of people. I have never broken down since, but I came close during one marvellous family reunion. I could feel myself going, so I quickly called for a commercial break and managed to pull myself together.' *(Scope Features)*

(Right) Cilla as a Southern belle with Bob Carolgees on Surprise, Surprise. 'When we are filming in winter and I go on a Cilla-gram date for Surprise, Surprise I wear a thick thermal vest and knickers under my posh frock to keep warm.'

(London Weekend Television)

(Above) 'When long-lost relatives have been reunited on Surprise, Surprise they need care, and we have a back-up system to help them, to see them through the trauma. Sometimes they don't get on well together, and have different views about life.'

(London Weekend Television)

1985

PLAYING CUPID

HIGHLIGHTS

20 FEBRUARY	**10th concert tour in Australia**
28 JUNE	**Pilot TV show for Blind Date**
7 JULY	**1st of 7 concerts**
20 SEPTEMBER	**'There's a Need in Me' released**
7 OCTOBER	**Album 'Surprisingly Cilla' released**
14 OCTOBER	**Concert tour of the Middle East**
30 NOVEMBER	**Blind Date TV series begins**
DECEMBER	**'Surprise, Surprise' single released**
22 DECEMBER	**3rd Surprise, Surprise TV series begins**

Alan Boyd, controller of entertainment at LWT in 1985, said that his first series of Surprise, Surprise had been tantamount to piloting an important programme in peak time with no protection against the knockers. 'Some of the earliest ones went out live; we knew certain strands were wrong but they couldn't be reworked fast enough. A lot of arguing and persuading went on. By the second series, Cilla understood what we were out to achieve and had educated herself to deal with her new role. Also, we had taken out the rubbish.'

Cilla

On Surprise, Surprise, a girl named Janet Pemberton drove her Datsun car through a shop window – a stunt: the window was made of stunt glass and all the TVs and stereos Janet plunged into were cardboard dummies. I was dead jealous of Janet. I have this thing about smashing things myself. In fact, if someone were to offer me a surprise treat the one I would choose would be to smash my best dishes. Mind you, I wonder what Bobby would have to say. Really, though, I don't want any surprises, thank you very much. I would hate to be surprised. I'd go berserk, I just don't like the idea of being caught unprepared. I know what goes into surprising people on the show, all that hush, hush, under-the-table stuff. I do love springing surprises on other people – the planning, and seeing their faces

'I can tell immediately if the Blind Date couples will hit it off. You can see it in their eyes when they come face to face from behind the screen. Many's the time a contestant has whispered to me: "I wish I'd picked the blonde girl instead" or "The bloke I chose looks the worst of the three". The boys are much cheekier to me than the girls. Maybe they sense they can have a good laugh with me.'
(Scope Features)

when I spring my treat on them. But I don't want any part of that myself … unless it's a nice treat for Christmas.

Meanwhile, lying on a shelf at LWT were sample tapes of Blind Date, versions of the show made and shown successfully in different territories abroad. Programme bosses in London had yet to figure out a way of reworking the format to suit the ITV family audience. Duncan Norvelle featured in a pilot which producers decided was too sex-orientated for the UK. Cilla saw the pilot – 'I watched it as a viewer rather than an artist with Bobby and I cried my eyes out with laughter and thought it was very funny' – but although she was convinced that Blind Date was a hit show, she had yet to be persuaded that it was for her.

Cilla

When I did the pilot the television watchdogs of the IBA were wary of the programme. They worried about the sexual connotations. Some of the American shows were quite raunchy. They asked me to front the programme, saying, 'We want you to do it because we tried to think of the most sexless person on television – and came up with your name'! I've never been on a blind date myself in my life, although when I was working in a Liverpool office, answering the telephone, occasionally a blind date would be suggested.

The eventual decision that Cilla should be the star of Blind Date was taken with perfect timing. The first batch of seven shows began to go out just ahead of a third series of Surprise, Surprise. At the end of that year Cilla was to be seen on the box for longer each week than anyone else except the newsreaders.

Cilla

There's a lot of snobbery about Blind Date. People won't admit to watching it, but they do. In our time we've already beaten Coronation Street – my own favourite programme – in the ratings. Everyone I know loves Blind Date.

People who come on the show are totally new to television, so in case they freeze up in front of the cameras they're given some idea of what they might be asked.

(Left) Sarah Evans, central figure in Cilla's Circle Of Fans, kept this shot of the singer seen on stage at Bournemouth's Pavilion Theatre in July 1985. *(Sarah Evans)*

(Far left) Frankie Howerd: 'You'd have to be blind to go on a date with 'er!' *(London Weekend Television)*

1986

A FLAIR FOR PANTO

HIGHLIGHTS

23 MARCH   **1st of 3 concert dates**

21 JULY   **Summer season, Futurist Theatre, Scarborough**

30 AUGUST   **2nd Blind Date TV series begins**

18 DECEMBER   ***Aladdin* pantomime, Empire Theatre, Liverpool**

28 DECEMBER   **Surprise, Surprise TV special**

Veteran theatrical director and producer Dickie Hurran came out of semi-retirement for Cilla's *Aladdin* at the Liverpool Empire at the end of 1986. 'Cilla's special talent for panto is that common touch, that smashing ability to communicate with people,' he enthused. Hurran explained that he had enjoyed a twenty-year working relationship with Cilla, producing both spectacular summer shows and Christmas pantomimes for her: 'When it comes to contact, she is the finest woman performer of her type, the best since Gracie Fields, and I'm old enough to have seen Gracie many times. Cilla never tries to be anybody else. She'll play the cockney boy Dick Whittington quite happily with a Scouse accent.'

Said Hurran: 'Cilla establishes the same rapport with an audience in Oxford or Bristol or here on Merseyside. Having her own family helps enormously. She loves children and is a great favourite with them. She brings out things in kids which she knows will amuse the parents. The main object is to make sure the kids are entertained. Their enjoyment is something the adults are perfectly happy to share.'

Cilla

I love babies and all that babies involve, but I'm not very good when they reach puberty. I'm a bit of a prude. I got intimidated when Robert and Ben made remarks about topless girls on the beach. Some of the things Bobby and the boys discuss really embarrass me. But I'm thankful Bobby is so open with them.

Hurran recalled a classic moment from Cilla's pantomime career. 'Once, as Dick

Whittington, Cilla had been banished and was walking all the way to Highgate. Her feet were sore and the Cat was tired. She told Puss they had another forty miles to go and he looked to the audience for sympathy. "Carry him, Cilla!" shouted a little boy in the crowd. Quick as a flash, Cilla came back with: "Carry him? I've already carried three kids, Robert John, Ben and our Jack, I'm not going to start carrying a big cat at my time of life!" The roof was raised. Panto is a perfect showplace for the unscripted gag and Cilla is the ideal performer when it comes to ad lib.'

Cilla

In December 1986 when I opened in *Aladdin* at the Liverpool Empire I was given the full treatment by young Merseyside fans. It was thanks to Blind Date, I think. All those teenyboppers thought I was superwoman or something. It was just like the sixties when teenagers used to grab the buttons of my Mary Quant plastic mac.

NME cover – 15 November 1986. (*NME*)

1987

PRIZE-WINNING PERSONALITY

HIGHLIGHTS

18 JANUARY	**4th Surprise, Surprise TV series begins**
3 FEBRUARY	**Named ITV Personality of 1986 at Variety Club awards**
22 FEBRUARY	**Named Favourite Female Television Personality of 1986 at *TV Times* awards ceremony**
14 MARCH	**11th concert tour of Australia**
24 JUNE	**Compères Birthright Royal Charity Gala, London Palladium**
13 JULY	**Summer season, Congress Theatre, Eastbourne**
5 SEPTEMBER	**3rd Blind Date TV series begins**
20 SEPTEMBER	**1st of 6 concert dates**
27 DECEMBER	**Surprise, Surprise TV special**

Apart from her summer season consisting of around forty stage shows at Eastbourne's Congress Theatre, the number of concert performances which Cilla gave in 1987 matched up more or less equally to the number of television shows she made via her fourth series of Surprise, Surprise, which included a Christmas special, and her third series of Blind Date, which ran for seventeen weeks.

Cilla

I know that Blind Date makes compulsive viewing when they are rude to each other but I do wish more would hit it off. Sometimes they can be quite vicious. One girl hated the guy she had chosen so much that she said at the end of the show, 'The only way I would like to meet him again would be through a medium.' The poor fellow asked me afterwards, 'Surely, Cilla, I'm not grotesque. I was out with Miss Wales at the weekend.'

Another girl almost burst into tears after her blind date told 18 million viewers, 'She's a pukka Sloane desperate to be an A-division yuppie.' The girl was extremely upset because she never suspected he despised her so much. Our show isn't meant to be sexy. It's just a bit of a giggle, and the couples get the chance of a lovely holiday. They can be unlucky, though, and end up windsurfing on the Manchester waterway.

'It might come as a surprise to some viewers but I am still a singer,' Cilla said as she and Bobby flew out of London's Heathrow Airport on 5 March to begin her latest tour of Australia. On the way home the following month, they stopped off in Honolulu where Robert, Ben and Jack joined them for an Easter holiday.

The year brought two significant awards: the Variety Club of Great Britain named Cilla ITV Personality and readers of *TV Times* voted her Favourite Female TV Personality.

(Above) Taking a bow on stage at the Liverpool Empire: Cilla with Bob Carolgees and Gareth Hunt in *Aladdin*.
(Sarah Evans)
(Left) Cilla and her Spitting Image alter ego help to launch ITV's 1987 Christmas programming package.
(Rex Features)

1988

SILVER JUBILEE

HIGHLIGHTS

10 JANUARY	**5th Surprise, Surprise TV series begins**
20 JANUARY	**Named Favourite Female Television Personality of 1987 at *TV Times* awards ceremony**
SPRING	**Heinz Baked Beans TV commercial**
24 MAY	**Named Most Popular TV Performer at Royal Television Society's awards**
29 MAY	**Special edition of Blind Date for ITV Telethon**
3 SEPTEMBER	**4th Blind Date TV series begins**
17 SEPTEMBER	**Cilla Celebrates 25 Years concert, Royal Festival Hall, London**
16 OCTOBER	**Desert Island Discs**
1 DECEMBER	**Birthright Lunch for Life**

Could it really be a quarter of a century since Cilla stood stiffly in the centre of the vast stage at London's Finsbury Park Astoria as a guest in The Beatles' Christmas Show of 1963 and sang Paul McCartney's 'Love of the Loved'? Cilla's silver jubilee concert at London's Royal Festival Hall in September 1988 was combined with a behind-the-scenes get-together of her Circle of Fans, at which members met her and chatted about the show. It was a novel way of marking her twenty-fifth anniversary.

The concert, staged in association with BBC Radio 2 and featuring guests Frankie Howerd, George Martin and Vince Hill, took the form of a potted history of Cilla's musical career to date. In front of the luxurious sound of a sixty-five strong BBC concert orchestra she sang 'It's for You', 'You've Lost that Lovin' Feelin'', 'Alfie', 'Step Inside Love' and 'Something Tells Me', chattering informally about the old days with conductors Ronnie Hazlehurst and

TV Times cover, 3 September 1988. (*TV Times*) (Left) Cilla's Circle Of Fans twenty-fifth Anniversary Souvenir Brochure.

CILLA BLACK
1963 – 1988

25th Anniversary Souvenir

(Left) Silver Jubilee concert at the Royal Festival Hall: Cilla Celebrates 25 Years with one of her best showbiz friends, Frankie Howerd. *(Philip Polglaze)*

(Middle) Tiers and laughter: LWT hosted a twenty-fifth anniversary lunch for Cilla on 26 September 1988. *(Rex Features)*

(Bottom) Cilla at Birthright's charity Lunch For Life on 1 December 1988, an occasion graced by the presence of Princess Diana. 'I frequently get asked to appeal for charities because I am Cilla Black, but this time it is also because I am personally involved. I am one of the women Birthright could help. I know what it is like to have a baby who dies. It is a shattering experience that we hope one day no woman will have to go through.' *(Syndication International)*

George Martin. She even sang 'Love of the Loved' for the first time since the sixties. Finally she closed with 'I Just Called to Say I Love You', 'You'll Never Walk Alone' and 'You're My World'. After that the bouquets came in thick and fast from all quarters, and Cilla's face was one mass of smiles and tears.

During 1988 Cilla won the *TV Times* award as Female Television Personality Of The Year for the second time. She also received the new Popular Arts award from the Royal Television Society.

Cilla

In the post-show party after Blind Date I've had to slap a few wrists and tell the lads to put the girls down. Everyone gets on great except the people going off on the blind date together.

When the show is being made, it's great television, of course, if they slag each other off, but if it's pure venom it's upsetting. I love it when they do get along. All the contestants are amazing. They're potential stars. I just sit back and let them take over.

Before the recording I do visit some of them in the studio. They get a bit nervous, waiting on their own, so I pop along in my dressing-gown and make them feel at home. I insult the fellas and look after the girls. I'm a bit of a feminist on that side. I've always been in a man's world, having three brothers and three sons.

All the men would rather be the pickers than the ones being picked. They say they can't take being turned down in front of their mates. Women are more relaxed about it, and don't take it so seriously.

1989

THE NAME OF THE ROSE

HIGHLIGHTS

6 JANUARY	**6th Surprise, Surprise TV series begins**
15 FEBRUARY	**Named Favourite Female Television Personality of 1988 at** *TV Times* **awards ceremony**
11 APRIL	**Named IBA TV Personality of the Year at TV and Radio Industries Club lunch**
4 JUNE	**Appears at Home Town charity show, Empire Theatre, Liverpool**
29 JULY	**Best of Blind Date**
16 SEPTEMBER	**5th Blind Date TV series begins**
22 DECEMBER	***Aladdin* pantomime, Wimbledon Theatre, London**
31 DECEMBER	**Cilla's Goodbye to the Eighties TV show**

In 1989 Cilla was given the *TV Times* award for the third consecutive year and was also voted ITV Personality of the Year by the Television and Radio Industries Club (TRIC). A racehorse and a Chelsea Flower Show rose were named after her and she took part in an all-star concert in Liverpool to aid victims of the Hillsborough soccer stadium disaster. Such fame is not without its minor irritation when it comes to the ordinary things in life, however …

Cilla

I'm intrigued by the property columns in newspapers. Often I'll ring up people about the homes they're selling. I try to disguise my voice, but people still recognise it's me. It's awful when I want a leg wax, or if I talk to a plumber about a leak in the shower, people just burst out laughing and say 'Surprise, Surprise'. This was funny at first, but now I get a bit annoyed. It's even more frustrating when the person I'm speaking to thinks it isn't me on the other end of the line, but someone imitating me.

As final confirmation of Cilla's undoubted status as the decade's First Lady of British television, she was given the prestigious job of hosting ITV's New Year's Eve programme, entitled Cilla's Goodbye to the Eighties.

Publicising her panto: Cilla returned to Wimbledon in December 1989 to repeat her favourite Christmas role of Aladdin. *(Rex Features)*

Home is where the heart is: Cilla and Bobby celebrated twenty years of marriage in 1989. 'I'm totally faithful to Bobby. I've never had an affair and I've never been tempted.

'If any woman wants a happy marriage she should marry a Scouser. They might be poor, but they'll always laugh about it.

'I know a lot of talented ladies who are not as lucky as me, because I have Bobby. You can get agents and TV people forever telling you how wonderful you are. But when we get home it's down to a bit of straight talking. Our home and the family are the greatest things in our lives. Once those electronic gates close behind us it's just Mr and Mrs Willis.

'Our kids are what we work for, and if we can't be together as a proper family, what's the point? Bobby and I never take our rows to bed. Once we get between the sheets, that's it. We have a big rule that no matter how big an argument we've had there's no dragging the blankets and pillows into the living room to sleep on the sofa. I don't think we'll ever stop loving each other. Bobby's so warm and patient – a real Prince Charming.' *(Scope Features)*

PART 4

the nineties

(London Weekend Television/Terry O'Neill)

1990

PANDA-ING TO THE AUSSIES

HIGHLIGHTS

FEBRUARY **Named Favourite Female Television Personality of 1989 by TV Times readers**

16 FEBRUARY **7th Surprise, Surprise TV series begins**

29 SEPTEMBER **6th Blind Date TV series begins**

12 NOVEMBER **Album 'Cilla's World' released (Australia only)**

26 NOVEMBER **Night of 100 Stars charity concert, London Palladium**

8 DECEMBER **Hosts Happy Birthday Coronation Street**

11 DECEMBER **Cilla's Christmas Lunch, Variety Club lunch guest of honour, Hilton Hotel, London**

In terms of touring, throughout her thirty years in showbusiness, Australia has been Cilla's most important territory outside the UK. The combined popularity of her records and her television shows with fans Down Under has made her a sure-fire winner at concert and cabaret box offices.

At the beginning of the nineties, Cilla tailored a recording project specifically for the Australian market. The venture began with a phone call from Sydney. 'They asked me if I was interested in doing a children's album. They mentioned "green" and "the environment" and I got more and more interested.'

Behind the idea was exiled Londoner Joanne Petersen, an old friend from the sixties when she was Brian Epstein's private secretary. Joanne was now living in Australia as the wife of former Bee Gees drummer Colin Petersen and working for the music company MCA/Gilbey. Some songs were sent to Cilla.

Cilla
They were lovely. There was the very funny 'Penguin Strut' and a song about about a panda which brought a little tear to my eye was I finished listening to it for the first time. All the songs had a little message, they were all educational without being stuffy.

Cilla with Coronation Street star Julie Goodyear at a Downing Street showbusiness gathering on 19 March 1990. 'I would love to have been in Coronation Street. When I die, if I come back I want to come back as Bet Lynch. I'm such a big fan.' *(Sun)*

'I'm so lucky. I've got everything I ever dreamed of, and I'm not ashamed to admit that I do say a prayer every night – thank you very much, God.

'I've got used to having money now and I like having it. I like buying frocks and drinking champagne. I'm a capitalist. I've never apologised for it. Why should I? I support the Conservatives because I live like one. I'm not two-faced about it. There's no way I'm a champagne Socialist.' *(Press Association)*

'A Lorra Corra!' – Cilla hosted Granada Television's Happy Birthday Coronation Street on 8 December 1990. *(Granada Television)*

(Left) *Weatherfield Recorder*: 'Happy Birthday Coronation Street'. *(Granada Television)*

Sold on the idea of such an unusual concept, Bobby and Cilla agreed to go ahead with an album of sixteen original children's songs under the title 'Cilla's World', all written by Playschool's Don Spencer. The recording sessions, produced in London by Rod Edwards, brought Cilla back into 'hands on' working contact with George Martin, who supervised the making of the album.

Launching 'Cilla's World', George Martin said: 'From the first moment I met her when she was a teenager, through those early heady days of Number One records, right to the present time, when she's the biggest television star in the country today, with programmes like Blind Date and Surprise, Surprise, we've been very good friends. I'm delighted that she's actually working on a project which is most timely because it's an album of children's songs, delightful songs, with animals and the environment. It couldn't be a better subject to choose today.' The album was released in Australia in November 1990.

On 11 December, Cilla was honoured at a pre-Christmas London Hilton luncheon of the Variety Club Of Great Britain, at which the speakers included chief barker Paul Gregg, Christopher Biggins, George Martin, former BBC supremo Bill Cotton and Frankie Howerd.

Responding to their words of praise and congratulation, Cilla talked about her many recording experiences with George Martin as producer, singling out the sessions with Burt Bacharach for 'Alfie' as a special highlight. She told Bill Cotton that he was the man to blame for her being on television at all, because he'd had the faith in her to produce the first Cilla series.

Cilla also spoke of her long and very close friendship with Frankie Howerd, which had started in 1966 ('Since when he has lusted after me all these years!'). Becoming more serious and a little emotional, Cilla expressed her special appreciation to Frankie for the invaluable support and counselling he had provided on personal and family matters over the years, most recently in connection with a motor accident of Robert's. A few months later at a similar Variety Club event in honour of Frankie Howerd, the tables were turned and Cilla was one of those chosen to talk about the veteran comic's extraordinary talent and achievements.

Blind Date

Cilla

At the beginning I was not all that happy to host Blind Date because I'm a singer and never felt I was any good with the rehearsed comic patter. I'm not a comedienne. I never work out lines before I go on. It just comes naturally. I did try to stick to a script, but it came across very false.

'Ooh eh! Who got you ready, chuck?' A scene from the sixth series of Blind Date in May 1990. 'None of the lads on the Blind Date show tries to chat me up in a serious way but we have a lorra fun. I'm like a mother hen to them. With all that talent there I don't stand a chance.

'When the contestants relax together after a show, over a drink, what seems like a budding romance on the air often just fizzles out. It amazes me that the pickers and those they've picked are never together after the show. They're always chatting up the ones they didn't pick.

'I remember one elderly couple, George and Edith, who featured in a Christmas episode of Blind Date. That Edith! She's the one person I know who could run me out of rabbit. She prattled on and on. I was crying with laughter so much one of my false eyelashes fell off.' *(London Weekend Television)*

'After seeing Blind Date in Australia, where it's called Perfect Match, and later in America, where it's called The Dating Game, I told London Weekend, "You've just gorra get this on the air."' *(London Weekend Television)*

Cilla
No, I've never been on a blind date myself. I never had the bottle. I thought they might turn out like Quasimodo.

Cilla
One of the fascinations of Blind Date is that it's a situation that we've all been involved within real life. When you're young someone is always trying to fix you up with a blind date. It's always someone who looks like Steve McQueen and has pots of money, they say. He usually turns out to be a long streak who couldn't even pay for the picture!

Cilla

One reason Blind Date is so successful is that the kids on the show aren't frightened of me. We'd never get the show on the road if I had too powerful an image, although sometimes I do wish I had an image that wasn't as common as muck. I've always had this guilt feeling because of my background and my poor Dad. I remember when I was young, when anyone talked posh I tried to talk posh because people weren't used to the Liverpool accent. I tried it and kept putting in aitches where there weren't supposed to be any. I soon got rid of that. Nowadays it's like me as I am or lump it.

(Below) First dates? Children featured in Cilla's 1992 Blind Date Christmas Special. 'In July 1992 we did the first junior version of Blind Date for the ITV Telethon. It was the youngsters themselves who persuaded me to do it. The only problem for the producers was finding enough boys. We knew before we started there'd be more girls than boys writing in. You know what boys are like at that age – they don't want to know about girls and all that romantic stuff.' (London Weekend Television)

(Above) 'Oh, my hat, what a wedding!' Cilla with her Blind Date bride and groom on 19 October 1991. 'In October 1991 when Blind Date contestants Alex Tatham and Sue Middleton got married after meeting on the show two years earlier I was thrilled. They were an incredible couple – so different. He went to Eton. She was from Birmingham and quite stunning. She reminded me of Farrah Fawcett. I wished them a lorra, lorra luck.

'Wild horses wouldn't have kept me away from that wedding. My first thought was to get a really smashing hat, and then I realised that it's the bride and bridegroom's mothers who wear the marvellous hats. So I chose something a bit different – and what a lot of stick I got afterwards! People have never stopped reminding me of it.' (London Weekend Television)

(Right) Some surprising contestants celebrated the 100th episode of Blind Date in September 1991. *(London Weekend Television)*

(Below) Senior Citizens Special, an ever-popular occasional feature of Blind Date. 'Soon after Blind Date started, I began to get loads of letters from pensioners saying "What about us!" and my heart went out to them. I love old people. They're so patient and have got so many funny stories to tell.

'Our first couple, Elvie and Gerald, brought the house down. They were fantastic and so raunchy. Gerald said the greatest thing about it was that he'd made a friend. They talked non-stop, they had so much in common.

'On the 1986 Blind Date Christmas Special, Edith from Lancashire – a pensioner – was a picker. She was wonderful. Her date said that marriage had crossed his mind and her reply was "Oh no, I don't want to wash any more dirty underpants."' *(London Weekend Television)*

Cilla

I suppose it's a bit difficult to start a romance on Blind Date when a couple are being followed by a camera crew all the time. Most of our couples don't get on anyway. What happens on the show is that the girl picks the fellow because of his voice. But they boys listen to what the girl is saying about herself. Often I want to scream to the girl 'Don't pick him!' but I've got to stop myself.

1991

BUYING A HAT

HIGHLIGHTS

7 JANUARY	**Appears at Cliff Richard Concert, Wembley Arena, London**
9 FEBRUARY	**Named Favourite Female Television Personality of 1990 at *TV Times* awards ceremony**
22 FEBRUARY	**8th Surprise, Surprise TV series begins**
7 SEPTEMBER	**7th Blind Date TV series begins**
19 OCTOBER	**Attends 1st Blind Date wedding**
13 DECEMBER	***Jack and the Beanstalk* pantomime, Piccadilly Theatre, London**

Cilla was thrilled when the first Blind Date wedding took place in 1991.

Cilla

My advice to anyone coming on Blind Date? If you're seeking a marriage partner, this is not your opportunity! Blind Date is an entertainment show for having fun, and if you did happen to find an ideal mate, that would be a bonus. The idea, though, is to come on it hoping you'll get some laughs and a nice holiday. The very bottom of the list is finding a prospective husband or prospective wife.

Regarding the first couple who did get together and get married through Blind Date, no dating agency would have put those two together but, as it happens, they were two nice, well-suited people.

At Christmas 1991, Cilla returned to London's West End, specifically to the Piccadilly Theatre, to star in more than fifty performances of *Jack and the Beanstalk*, directed and staged by Tudor Davies, with Bob Carolgees and Spit the Dog, Patrick Mower and Bread's Jean Boht as the Fairy.

'I've been a member of Cliff Richard's fan club for thirty years. I'm a fully paid-up member, but they've made me an honorary member now.'
(*Express Newspaper plc*)

(Below) Cilla with Bobby holding her Variety Club Showbusiness Personality of 1991 Award. 'I daren't think what would happen if Bobby were not here to share things with. Heaven knows what rubbish I'd have accepted in the past if Bobby hadn't been there to advise. Without him I'd have no choice but to retire from showbusiness.

'If I couldn't look across a room and see his reassuring face I'd die inside. In business, no one could match Bobby. He negotiates everything for me. Yet though he's a good businessman, and always gets the best for me, no one ever resents him. In fact at London Weekend Television I think the people like him more than they like me!'

(*Press Association/Tony Harris*)

(Left) *Jack and the Beanstalk*, Piccadilly Theatre – programme. 'My *Jack and the Beanstalk* panto opened on 13 December 1991 and ran till 19 January 1992 at the Piccadilly Theatre, London. The producers were dead crafty. They asked me the previous summer if I'd do it for them. As a result I was busy working through Christmas and New Year while the producers were sunning themselves in Florida! I'm only kidding. I find panto exciting. And thank goodness I've got good legs to show off. It's great to hear the kids scream with glee and hear them shout "Kill 'im" when the Baddie appears.'

Champagne 'n' rain: Cilla renews her LWT contract on 14 March 1991. *(London Weekend Television)*

'Bobby has a wonderful voice and turned down a recording contract. He's the most selfless person I know, and the one I trust most. If I've done a show and everyone is telling me how terrific it was, I always look at Bobby and if he doesn't give his seal of approval I know I could have done better.

'I often think there's a book in Bobby, if only he'd write it! His life has been so interesting. When he was eleven and his mother died, with his father out of work he starting cooking for the whole household.

'Today he does most of the weekend cooking at our house too. He also does his own ironing, and our sons, having seen their father at the ironing board, also iron their own shirts. I'm the one who does the washing, though. I'm a perfect candidate for the washing powder ads.

'I'm lucky that Bobby's also a good businessman. He's the one who negotiates my fees! We're together 24 hours a day, which would probably drive some people potty, and in the early days it did have a bad effect on us, leading to rows. But now, being together all the time makes us happy. If we do have a row I'm devastated because, I suppose, I'm so reliant on Bobby.' *(London Features International)*

1992

THIRTY YEARS YOUNGER

HIGHLIGHTS

4 FEBRUARY	**Named Showbusiness Personality of the Year at Variety Club awards**
12 FEBRUARY	**Presents Best British Album award at BRIT awards ceremony**
4 APRIL	**9th Surprise, Surprise TV series begins**
AUTUMN	**Allied Carpets TV commercial**
10 OCTOBER	**8th Blind Date TV series begins**
26 OCTOBER	**Performs at 40 Glorious Years concert to celebrate HM Queen's 40th jubilee**
25 DECEMBER	**Junior Blind Date Christmas special**

Back from a fortnight's post-panto holiday in Barbados in the first week of February 1992, a well-bronzed Cilla collected her Showbusiness Personality of the Year trophy from the Variety Club at another London Hilton Hotel luncheon.

The following month she took part in a unique TV project, publicising a £15,000,000 fund-raising appeal, Trading Places, to finance a ground-breaking breast cancer research centre. The idea was that famous celebrities should be seen trading places, so that Cilla, for example, switched Blind Date roles and played a partner-seeking contestant while outrageously OTT Julian Clary took her place as presenter.

Before the end of 1992, Cilla had already begun to anticipate how she'd feel at fifty in the forthcoming year that would mark her thirtieth anniversary in showbusiness.

Cilla

I'm really dreading it. I don't like getting old because I don't feel old. I still feel twenty, but I know that life is running away from me, and I'm not in control of it. I don't know where the last thirty years have gone. But I know I've worked hard and enjoyed every minute of it.

I'm very aware of keeping as healthy as I can. And although I love food I have to be

Cilla and Bobby in their conservatory at Denham. *(Rex Features/Conrad Hafenrichter)*

disciplined because my job calls for it. But on the day I retire this diet routine will stop. A fortune teller I met at a party in Spain in 1972 read my palm and told me I'd be semi-retired in five years. Me? I was shocked. I couldn't believe I was going to retire so soon. But, I thought, if that's the way it's going to be, that's the way it's going to be. That's fate.

Talking about her twenty-three-year-old marriage to Bobby, she said: 'We're more in love now than when we first married. He's the reason for me being here.' Confessing that neither of them could put hand on heart and say that they didn't get on each other's nerves sometimes, Cilla added: 'We do, and we row, but it's not often and it's nothing major.'

Cilla

When I'm upset Bobby always keeps my pecker up. If you lost your right arm he'd think of twenty reasons why you didn't need it anyway. Our marriage is successful because we've both had great upbringings and come from the same kind of family life. We all love one

another. We may have a mansion in Denham, set in seventeen acres, but I still think of myself as a Scouser.

I'm a lousy party hostess. I serve everyone champagne cocktails so they don't realise the dinner is burned. I wish my mother had taught me to cook. I'd rather go in front of 20 million television viewers live than give a dinner party. Luckily Bobby is a good cook.

We've got six baths in our house. Well, I'm only a docker's daughter from Liverpool and I used to wash in the tin bath in front of the fire on a Friday night. I suppose I'm over-compensating.

I have a room in our house where I store all my clothes. I'm a hoarder – never throw anything away. I hoard Bobby's clothes, too. Shoes are a special weakness. I've got one pair which cost £900. They're set with pieces of diamanté. At that price it should be real diamonds.

In 1992, Robert, now twenty-two years old, left Oxford University, having earned a BA degree with Honours in English and History, and took his first job ('He's working for Bob Geldof making coffee'). Meanwhile Ben, four years younger, was tackling his A-levels.

Cilla

I can't wait to be a granny. I think I'll make a much better granny than I did a mum. I see all these baby adverts on the telly and it makes me broody.

We're a very close family and I think my children have handled my TV fame very well. The biggest insult I ever had was when my son Ben switched from my programme on television to the other channel and watched Basil Brush instead.

Our children have been taught to earn their pocket money. For instance, our Robert decorated my mum's house in Liverpool in his spare time.

Once our Jack dropped his ice-cream on the floor and our dog ate it. Later he told me, 'I got my own back on the dog, Mum. When he wasn't looking I drank his water.'

(Far left) Cilla with Eurodisney's Mickey and Minnie Mouse, March 1992. *(Rex Features)*

(Left) 'Robert got his BA degree in English and History in 1992 and then started work working for Bob Geldof, making coffee. Then he started to work in television. We saw him one day on TV holding an umbrella over some presenter. I was only interested in whether he had a clean shirt on and had combed his hair.'

(Right) 40 Glorious Years: Cilla meets Prince Charles in the cast presentation line-up at the Earls Court concert to celebrate the Queen's jubilee. *(Rex Features/Nils Jorgensen)*

1993

A NEW LOOK

HIGHLIGHTS

12 MARCH	**Appears on BBC TV's Comic Relief, Mr Bean on Blind Date**
18 MARCH	**Begins recording 'Through the Years' album**
28 MARCH	**Sings with Barry Manilow at his Royal Albert Hall, London, concert**
25 APRIL	**10th Surprise, Surprise TV series begins**
9 MAY	**Unveils plaque to Frankie Howerd for Dead Comics Society**
27 MAY	**50th birthday**
SEPTEMBER	**30th Anniversary TV special**
2 OCTOBER	**9th Blind Date TV series begins**
15 NOVEMBER	**Hosts and tops the bill at the Royal Variety Show**

Cilla predicted more than once through the years that she would retire in 1993 at the age of fifty. But when it came to the crunch, there was no chance.

Cilla

How could I? There was this book, there was the new album, a TV special, the Royal Variety, and umpteen more series of Blind Date to be done!

I used to keep saying to Bobby that I'd jack it all in when I turned fifty and he just looked up to heaven because he knew there was no way I'd do that. I'll be singing into a hairbrush in front of the mirror when I'm seventy. I'll never give up, I'll make more comebacks than Frank Sinatra.

As Cilla began to record her latest series of eighteen new episodes of Blind Date for transmission from the beginning of October 1993, LWT announced that her show, their top Saturday entertainment production, was getting a facelift. The refurbishments included new titles, a new set, a new theme tune arrangement and a new series producer, Thelma McGough.

If Cilla let her fiftieth birthday slip past in relatively low profile, the same could not be said

Cilla's new look for the autumn of 1993: John Swannell took the picture as part of a special session for *Through the Years.* **(Sony Music/John Swannell)**

of her spectacularly celebrated thirtieth anniversary in showbusiness, an occasion marked not only by her acceptance of an invitation to host and perform in the 1993 Royal Variety Performance for ITV but by a number of projects, including this book, a freshly produced album, a home video cassette, and an LWT Special, all depicting aspects of the same theme: Cilla Through the Years.

The concept was first discussed in March 1991 over an exploratory lunch at a Chinese restaurant in King's Road, Chelsea, between Cilla and Bobby, Cilla's long-time agent John Ashby and Rick Blaskey, one half of The Music And Media Partnership which also includes composer/producer/arranger Charlie Skarbek.

Cilla with Barry Manilow and The Music and Media Partnership's Rick Blaskey, left, and Charlie Skarbek, producers of *Through the Years*. (London Weekend Television/Mike Vaughan)

The gist of Rick's proposal to Cilla in 1991 was that the Partnership should make a definitive Cilla Black album for the nineties, a programme of songs with lyrics which Cilla's widespread audience would relate to and/or remember with great affection. Rick explained: 'Cilla is a brilliant communicator – and bringer-together of people, a performer with exceptional powers of communication. This was not to be merely Surprise, Surprise: The Album but a collection of melodious, beautifully recorded songs from a range of sources, some already well-loved both by Cilla and her public, some entirely new ones conceived specifically for this venture.'

Cilla is known for having an immediate answer to everything when she is interviewed but during the lunch with Rick, she sat back and listened without jumping in.

Rick recalled: 'She was waiting for me to convince her that there was a market in the nineties for Cilla Black, the recording artist. She and Bobby knew it was not a question of getting an album recorded but of getting the right record company to market and promote it properly. I assured them that I would do a record deal calling for total commitment on the part of the company, otherwise we wouldn't go ahead at all.'

According to Rick, the anniversary connection was like 'icing on the cake'. The evocative album title came before the song of the same name had been composed. The lyrics of 'Through the Years' encapsulate the moods, emotions and memories of everyone who grew up alongside Cilla during her thirty years in showbusiness, forming (as she did) lasting friendships and lifelong musical tastes.

'Through the Years' by Charlie Skarbek and Rick Blaskey

Do you remember how it started way back then?
There were love songs on the radio and music became a friend,
Who'd have believed it but the melodies linger on,
They gave us inspiration and kept us goin' on.

They said that All You Need is Love;
Now we remember Yesterday.
The message was in the songs and the feelings were so strong
They sounded good and still sound good today.

Through the years we've dreamed our dreams together,
We hoped and prayed and some of them came true.
Through the years our memories live forever,
And like the music we made it through, through the years.

Do you remember in the movies
The hero reaches for his dream?
Whatever the hopes and fears through laughter and through tears,
The feelings just get stronger through the years.

For Cilla, the final add-on bonus was the chance to bring in professional friends and involve them one way or another in the creation of her conceptual celebration album.

Rick Blaskey commented, 'The choice of duet partners was simple. If the album was to be a musical extension of the Cilla that the public are so familiar with on TV, then it was clear that the choice of songs and duet partners should reflect the same warmth and feelings. Cliff Richard and Dusty Springfield have been friends with Cilla since the early years and Cilla is a

Cilla and Bazza: Cilla surprise surprised Barry Manilow on the stage of London's Royal Albert Hall during his concert on 28 March. He talked her into an impromptu duet – 'You'll Never Walk Alone'.
(Rex Features)

big fan of Barry Manilow – so invitations were extended to all three.'

Cilla and Barry searched for something compatible with both their singing styles and their musical backgrounds, a song containing what Rick calls a 'making it through and surviving' theme. They came up with 'You'll Never Walk Alone', which Cilla and Barry first performed together in public at London's Royal Albert Hall as part of an unrehearsed sequence for Surprise Surprise.

Cilla

Barry said that just because I hadn't used my singing voice as often in a recording studio during the last ten years didn't mean I'd lost anything: 'You've still got your voice, it's there, it hasn't gone away and it's not going to go away.' That was the most marvellous reassurance he could have given me and it was a great inspiration to me when I began to record.

Message from Barry Manilow

When I was eleven years old, my family took me to see my first Broadway musical. Even though we lived in Brooklyn, New York, the trip across the Brooklyn Bridge to Manhattan was always an exciting event for me. The show we saw was a revival of Rodgers and Hammerstein's *Carousel*.

As a youngster I had felt a connection with music but needed something to jump-start my motor and turn on my passion for music. 'You'll Never Walk Alone' was that jolt. When they sang this song at the end of the play, I remember feeling goosebumps rise all over my little eleven-year-old body. When I walked out of the theatre I had found the path I wanted to walk for the rest of my life.

Singing this song was a thrill.

Singing it with Cilla Black was an honour.

I'm extremely proud to be a part of this celebration of Cilla's career.

Barry Manilow

'That's What Friends Are For', Cilla's duet with Cliff Richard, resembles 'You'll Never Walk Alone' in that it depicts friendship which is true of Cliff and Cilla on a personal level and also true of what Cilla is all about in Blind Date and Surprise, Surprise.

Cilla with Cliff Richard. *(Sony Music/Tim Roney)*

Message from Cliff Richard

Thirty years – who would have thought it!

After all the decades that have flashed by, it's wonderful that we're still singing, and making and breaking records! Strangely enough, although we've sung many duets over the years, they've been mostly for TV and, until now, we've never had the chance of actually recording together.

So thank you for making another 'first' possible, and for inviting me to guest on your brand new album. May I wish you all the very best for its success – and all the best for everything you do. You are the best!

Love

Cliff Richard

Rather than going back to cover something from the sixties via her duet with Dusty Springfield, Cilla opted for a totally new song, 'Heart and Soul', which evokes the sound and image everyone has of the sixties while the lyrics are Cilla and Dusty talking in the nineties.

'Heart and Soul' by Charlie Skarbek and Rick Blaskey

It was back in '63, we were young and we were free,

Thought the world was really ours for the taking,

We had heart and we had soul, oh we lived for rock 'n' roll,

And didn't we, didn't we, didn't we do it?

Fashions come and fashions go, we were there so we should know,

I sometimes smile when I think of how I looked then,

Burnin' candles at both ends, hoping time would make amends,

And didn't we, didn't we, didn't we do it?

It seemed like there was nothing to it.

With heart and soul the world is yours, the stars are too,

If you bring out the best in you,

With heart and soul whatever you may want to do,

Heart and soul will see you through.

Now we're older nothing's changed, just some things are rearranged,

But the message is the same as when we started,

Gettin' stronger every day, looking back now we can say,

Didn't we, didn't we, didn't we do it?

It seemed like there was nothing to it.

Message from Dusty Springfield

When my manager, Vicki Wickham, rang to say I'd been asked to sing a duet with Cilla for her album, my immediate reaction was, 'Why not? It sounds like a lot of fun to me.' I love doing things that aren't blatantly obvious and I particularly enjoy duets. All I really had to do was to show up and sing in tune, which I actually did, amongst a sea of Thai food – Charlie runs a classy session! I'll sing for Charlie anytime if the food's that good.

I'd worked with Cilla before, liked her a lot, knew her to be a real pro, and felt that beneath the differences in style we'd give each other 'edge' and bring things out of each other which would work for the song. Happily I think the theory worked well and I hope the album is a smash for Cilla. She deserves it and besides, it was all a lorra laughs.

Dusty

Rick Blaskey described the other new song on the album 'A Dream Come True' as an optimistic universal but personal love song, and 'the best melody Andrew Lloyd Webber's never written'! Ralph McTell's haunting ballad 'Streets of London' was chosen as one of Cilla's personal favourites – McTell plays guitar on the track – and 'Will You Love Me

Tomorrow?' fell into the same category. At the time of his earliest meetings with Cilla, Rick had been working with Cliff Richard. He gave her a tape of 'From A Distance', a song he had also given to Cliff and which became a hit single for Cliff in 1990, and this was one of the first songs they agreed upon for Cilla's album. Although The Beatles had not been active as a band for twenty-three years, Cilla settled for the next best thing, a permanently popular song from the pens of John Lennon and Paul McCartney, 'Here, There and Everywhere'.

Cilla with Rowan Atkinson: in March, Mr Bean appeared in a spoof Comic Relief version of Blind Date for BBC Television. *(Rex Features/Richard Young)*

At first, Cilla wasn't at all sure about re-making 'Anyone Who Had a Heart' and 'You're My World'. Rick said: 'We had to twist her arm, she needed to be given a good reason for re-doing her biggest hits, the most prized nuggets from her musical past. The truth is that a whole new audience of people who watch her in the nineties don't know these classics in their original form. Bobby really helped to convince Cilla that they were such enduring songs and why wait for someone else eventually to do them; they were absolutely right to be brought into the nineties – and who better than by Cilla herself?' Neither 'You're My World' nor 'Anyone Who Had a Heart' has diminished or lost any of its magic in thirty years and eventually she agreed that if 'Through the Years' was to be a truly definitive Cilla Black album both titles belonged here. Rick added: 'We wanted to treat the two songs very faithfully, you don't touch such classics unless you can do them well, but Charlie also felt he could do a powerful contemporary production of each.' Charlie Skarbek's production brought Cilla's first two Number One hits into a nineties setting, using today's technology, and made them sound contemporary. It wasn't a matter of re-shaping so much as applying a new coat of paint.

In parallel with recording session plans, Rick and Cilla discussed a 'new look' for 'Through the Years' and a photo session with John Swannell was arranged at Broughton Castle, Oxford.

This took place in April 1993 and provided a set of very different pictures to be used on the front of this book and on the album cover. Before she was photographed, Cilla invited her hairdresser and longtime friend, Leslie Russell, out to Denham to talk about her 'new look'. Leslie said:

Her hair in his hands: Cilla has been a client and close friend of top London hair stylist Leslie Russell since Cathy McGowan introduced her to him in the sixties. Before having pictures taken for Through the Years in April, Cilla went to see Leslie at Smile, his salon in King's Road, Chelsea, and he gave her hair a new look.

(Sony Music/Tim Roney)

'We agreed that 'Through the Years' represented a milestone that ought to have a little message with it as far as hair fashion was concerned. In the event, I gave her a new haircut which was a shorter and more modern version of the layered look we did in the early seventies.'

The personal and professional relationship between Cilla and Leslie dates back to the sixties:

'I was introduced to Cilla at Ready, Steady, Go by a mutual client and mutual mate, television presenter Cathy McGowan. Cilla admired Cathy's long, shiny hair and they talked endlessly about fashion.' When Leslie opened what was claimed to be London's first unisex salon, Smile, in 1969, Cilla was among his many existing celebrity clients from Sandie Shaw to Michael Parkinson, who remained loyal. Soon afterwards he gave Cilla what he called the seventies layered page-boy look which became fashionable again in 1993:

'Blokes as well as girls used to ask Cilla who cut her hair because they wanted theirs like that, it was a unisex style. Even if they didn't know my name, people would ring up to book with "whoever does Cilla".

'Through the years, my job has been to understand images. A lot of people think Cilla's had the same cut but, if you study her pictures, you'll see a lot of changes. We were at loggerheads only once, when she wanted to be blonde and I've always liked her distinctive marmalade colouring. We used to do highlights in those

GRIFFIN'S EYE

"And you chose Number One, little Cilla from Liverpool."

Little Cilla caught Griffin's Eye: In April 1993, Cilla revealed first details of a cartoon show for television centred on an animated character she had created. She said: 'Little Cilla is an eleven-year-old who goes around getting on everyone's nerves. Her only friend is an Afghan hound called Chuck, who wears granny glasses and resembles John Lennon. On the cartoon show's soundtrack, I'll be doing the voice for Little Cilla. I'm really excited about this project.' On 26 April, the *Daily Mirror's* Griffin took up the idea that Little Cilla might become Britain's answer to the hit US cartoon series, The Simpsons, and produced a skit on Blind Date which brought together Cilla in her most successful television role, Bart Simpson, Little Cilla and her Afghan hound. *(By kind permission of the Daily Mirror)*

days and then put henna on the hair which gave it the marmalade effect. Cilla and Bobby came back from a long holiday in the Caribbean after spending so much time in the sun that her hair looked a lot lighter.

'Both Cilla and the television people wanted to stick with the blonde look. She insisted everybody liked it but me, so I let it run on for a while. I was very opposed to it and, like any hair stylist worth his salt, I won in the end and we went back to good old marmalade!'

Cilla has tended to surround herself with the same circle of associates and aides through the years, reliable people with whom not only working relationships but close friendships have formed, from the long-serving and indispensable Willis family nanny, Penny, to television producer Michael Hurll. Like Leslie Russell, Michael worked with Cilla all the way through from The Billy Cotton Show in the sixties to the tenth series of Surprise, Surprise in 1993.

After the recording of the final Surprise, Surprise show in 1993, Michael Hurll looked back:

'My first recollection, hers as well, is of telling Cilla off when she arrived late at the BBC for a rehearsal of The Billy Cotton Television Bandshow. I gave her a real dressing down and she didn't forget this. A few years later, when she was asked who she would like to produce her first BBC television series, she said immediately: "Michael Hurll". Her reasoning was that if I put the same degree of belief into Cilla as I had into The Billy Cotton Show I wouldn't stand for any nonsense from her guests!

Cilla with television producer Michael Hurll: spanning all four decades of Cilla's career, the successful working relationship between those two is among the longest in the industry. *(London Weekend Television/Mike Vaughan)*

'Cilla is a perfectionist with an in-built sense of what is right for her, an intuition that has never let her down. She is a truly charismatic star, one who knows how to take applause and how to approach every performance in a studio or on a stage with the same amount of professionalism. Such stars are rare in British showbusiness.

'I must also admit that through the years I have had more laughs with Cilla than with any other performer I have worked with.'

Thirty years ago a thin twenty-year-old Liverpool girl with a huge beehive of bright-red hair and a cheeky line in chatter to disguise her nervousness arrived in London to audition at EMI's famous Abbey Road recording complex, a white-knuckle experience for any youngster. This unassuming singer from Scotland Road, absolutely untutored in the crafts of a professional entertainer, stood stiffly in the middle of the studio floor with her arms pinned tightly to her sides at the elbows and belted out 'Love of the Loved' for The Beatles' record producer, George Martin.

In the beginning Cilla may have had The Fab Four's management team behind her but through the years she built her uniquely successful career on raw talent and sheer strength of personality, coupled with the rare and precious ability to communicate charmingly with any audience. Today she ranks as one of Britain's top television stars; tomorrow who knows what fresh surprises Cilla will spring on her millions of fans?

UK discography

Singles A Side/B Side	Label and Catalogue No.	Release Date	Highest Chart Position
Love of the Loved / Shy of Love	Parlophone R 5065	27 September 1963	35
Anyone Who Had a Heart / Just for You	R 5101	31 January 1964	1
You're My World / Suffer Now I Must	R 5133	1 May 1964	1
It's for You / He Won't Ask Me	R 5162	31 July 1964	7
You've Lost That Lovin' Feelin' / Is It Love?	R 5225	8 January 1965	2
I've Been Wrong Before / I Don't Want to Know	R 5265	15 April 1965	17
Love's Just a Broken Heart / Yesterday	R 5395	7 January 1966	5
Alfie / Night Time Is Here	R 5427	25 March 1966	9
Don't Answer Me / The Right One Is Left	R 5463	3 June 1966	6
A Fool Am I / For No One	R 5515	14 October 1966	13
What Good Am I? / Over My Head	R 5608	2 June 1967	24
I Only Live to Love You / From Now On	R 5652	17 November 1967	26
Step Inside Love / I Couldn't Take My Eyes Off You	R 5674	9 March 1968	8
Where Is Tomorrow? / Work is a Four-Letter Word	R 5706	7 June 1968	39
Surround Yourself With Sorrow / London Bridge	R 5759	7 February 1969	3
Conversations / Liverpool Lullaby	R 5785	27 June 1969	7
If I Thought You'd Ever Change Your Mind / It Feels So Good	R 5820	21 November 1969	20
Child of Mine / That's Why I Love You	R 5879	4 December 1970	-
Something Tells Me (Something's Gonna Happen Tonight) / La La La Lu	R 5924	15 November 1971	3
The World I Wish For You / Down In The City	R 5938	11 February 1972	-
You You You / Silly Wasn't I?	R 5972	17 November 1972	-
Baby We Can't Go Wrong / Someone	EMI 2107	4 January 1974	36
I'll Have to Say I Love You in a Song / Never Run Out	EMI 2169	24 May 1974	-
He Was a Writer / Anything You Might Say	EMI 2227	25 October 1974	-
Alfie Darling / Little Bit of Understanding	EMI 2278	28 March 1975	-
I'll Take a Tango / To Know Him Is to Love Him	EMI 2328	25 July 1975	-
Little Things Mean a Lot / It's Now	EMI 2438	12 March 1976	-
Easy in Your Company / I Believe	EMI 2532	September 1976	-
I Wanted to Call It Off / Keep Your Mind on Love	EMI 2658	15 July 1977	-
Silly Boy / I Couldn't Make My Mind Up	EMI 2791	12 May 1978	-
The Other Woman / Opening Night	EMI 2840	22 September 1978	-
There's a Need in Me / You've Lost That Lovin' Feelin'	Towerbell TOW 74	September 1985	-
Surprise, Surprise / Put Your Heart Where Your Love Is	TOW 81	December 1985	-

	Label and Catalogue No.	Release Date	
EPs			
Anyone Who Had a Heart	Parlophone GEP 8901	April 1964	
It's for You	GEP 8916	October 1964	
Cilla's Hits	GEP 8954	August 1966	
Time for Cilla	GEP 8967	June 1967	

	Label and Catalogue No.	Release Date	Highest Chart Position
Albums			
Cilla	Parlophone PMC 1243	25 January 1965	5
Cilla Sings a Rainbow	PMC 7004	18 April 1966	4
Sher-oo!	PMC 7041	6 April 1968	7
The Best of Cilla Black	PMC 7065	30 November 1968	21
Surround Yourself with Cilla	PCS 7079	23 May 1969	-
Sweet Inspiration	PCS 7103	3 July 1970	42
Images	PCS 7128	May 1971	-
Day by Day	PCS 7155	January 1973	-
In My Life	EMI 3031	7 June 1974	-
It Makes Me Feel Good	EMI 3108	March 1976	-
Modern Priscilla	EMI 3232	June 1978	-
Especially for You	K-TEL ONE 1085	3 August 1980	-
The Very Best of Cilla Black	Parlophone EMI TV 38	17 January 1983	20
Surprisingly Cilla	Towerbell TOWLP 14	7 October 1985	-

	Label and Catalogue No.	Release Date	
Budget Albums/Re-Issues			
Cilla	World Record Club ST 1036	1969	
Yesterday	ST 1100	1969	
You're My World	Regal Starline SRS 5044	1970	
25 Wonderful Tracks	Regal Starline EXE 1009	1972	
Step Inside Live (Sher-oo! re-issue)	Sounds Superb SPR 90019	1973	
Cilla Sings a Rainbow (re-issue)	SPR 90062	1973	
The Very Best of Cilla Black	Music For Pleasure MFP 41	1983	
Listen With Mother (one track only)	BBC Records 525	1984	
Love Songs (Especially for You re-issue)	K-TEL ONE 1355	1988	
25th Anniversary Album	Music For Pleasure DL 1134	1988	
Yesterday (re-issue)	C5 Records C5-547	1989	
The EMI Years – The Best of Cilla Black	EMI TCEMS 1410	1991	
Ladies of Pop (5 Cilla tracks)	Knight Records ltd KNCD 15014	1991	

(Rex Features/Nils Jorgensen)